THE BATTLE OF CULTURE

TEARING

DOWN

STRONGHOLDS

Rev. Anthony Martin

Author-Inspirational/Motivational

Evangelistic Speaker

**The Kingdom Culture Fellowship Ministries
& Christian Self Publishing Co.**

Copyright © 2014 ~ 2020 by Rev. Anthony Martin

THE BATTLE OF THE CULTURE
TEARING DOWN STRONGHOLDS
2nd EDITION
By REV. ANTHONY MARTIN
Printed in the United States of America

ISBN 978-1-63273-016-9

Unless otherwise indicated, Bible quotations are taken from

All rights reserved solely by the author. The author guarantees all contents are original and No part of this book may be reproduced in any form without the permission of the author. The views expressed in this book are not necessarily all those of the publisher.

Unless otherwise indicated, Bible quotations are taken from
The Kingdom Culture Exploratory Study Bible
The Kingdom English Standard Bible.
The Kingdom Culture Fellowship Ministries & Christian Self Publishing Co.

www.thekingdomcultureblog.com

This Book is dedicated to

THE
ONES
WHO
ENDURES

Contents

Preface iii
Introduction v

THE BATTLE OF THE CULTURE

1. The Triune Devil 7
2. The Kingdom of GOD vs. The Kingdom of Devil 41
3. Identity Crises 47
4. Religion vs. Science 57
5. Questioning GOD 84
6. War is Declared 125
7. Death and Destruction 146
8. The Signs of the Time 168
A Message to the Church

INTRODUCTION

The Word of GOD is the most powerful Knowledge, Understanding and Wisdom before us. The Word of GOD is and forever will be the most powerful Knowledge, Understanding and Wisdom before us. There is great mockery in saying man wrote the Word of GOD, and yes man was inspired by the presents of GOD to do just that, but to give man that level of credit in writing such a powerful Book of Law is beyond man's infinite wisdom. There is no way possible that man alone can write a Book to instruct man on how to live GOD, when man does not know the mind of GOD. Man has no clue of GOD's existence. The purpose for my book is to bring back excitement in reading GOD's word, this is not the Bible, and this book does not take the place of bible. This book is a reference book to study along with the bible to give you some great insight of Genesis to Revelations. This book will give you some insight of the spiritual warfare that we face in our daily lives as we go about our days. Devil and his death demons stay on the attack 24 hours a day and we have no business given GOD 2 to 3 hours of our time, when we are not here for our purpose. GOD gave us life, GOD gave us this Heaven and the Earth for us to manage for Him, He is CEO of Heaven and Earth. We are His employees, not His employer. Devil is already sentence to eternal death; all he seeks now is to take many of you with him for purposes of not being alone. Hell and the Lake of Fire was not set up for us, it is prepared for devil and his death demons only (Matt. 25: 41,) not us. So why would so many be headed there.

Introduction

This book is purposed to help many to avoid going along with devil and his death demons and to help you understand how things work in the Kingdom of God and the Kingdom of Devil. This book is to help you become a threat to the Devil's Kingdom that he will be reminded of where he is headed and to remind you of where you don't belong. This book will inform you of how things work from Genesis to Revelation in the Kingdom of Heaven as well as The Kingdom of GOD on Earth. It is in every Man, Woman and Child of GOD's contract (The Great Commission Matt 28; Mark 16:15-18) with the Kingdom of GOD to carry out His assignment given to each and every one of us. You must know your assignment that GOD gave you not what skills you so call have developed of the world and believe this is what you are suppose to be doing here on Earth. I am talking the GOD given assignment in which GOD placed in all to bring souls to Him through His Son Our Lord and Savior Jesus Christ. For those who are saved allow this book in book to enhance your Knowledge, Understand and Wisdom of the Word of GOD. For those of you who are not knowledgeable to the Kingdom of GOD then allow this book to enrich you to be well informed of The Almighty GOD and Our Lord and Savior Jesus Christ, and may His grace and mercy be with you, AMEN.

CHAPTER I

THE

TRIUNE DEVIL

SATAN

There are many who deny the existence of Satan. They claim that what we call Satan is only a "principle of evil." That this "evil" is sort malaria an intangible thing like disease germs that floats about in the atmosphere and attacks people's heart under certain conditions. The existence of Satan cannot be determined by the opinions of men. The only source of information is the Bible. That is the reason why Satan tries to discredit the word of God. He is not a "principle of evil" he is a— Person. "Be sober, be vigilant; because your adversary the Devil, as a lion, walks about, seeking whom he may devour." 1 Pet. 5:8. He walketh," he roareth," he is to be "chained," Rev. 20:1-3. These could not be said of a "principle of evil." He has many names or aliases— "Satan," "Devil," "Beelzebub," "Belial," "Adversary, ""Dragon," "Serpent." He is mentioned by one or the other of these names 174 times in the Bible. He is a great "Celestial Potentate." He is "the Prince of the Powers of the Air." Eph. 2:2. "The God of this World" (Age) 2 Cor. 4:4. He is the "God" not of the earth, for that belongs to its Maker—God. "The earth is the Lord's and the fullness thereof." Satan is the God of the "World Systems" of the habitable earth. These "World Systems" embrace business, society, politics and religion. Satan is the Ruler of the "Powers of Darkness" of the "Spirit World," (Eph. 6:11, 12), and his position is so exalted that even Michael the Archangel dare not insult him. Jude 9. So mighty is he that man cannot successfully resist him without Divine help I. **His Origin**, this is more or less shrouded in mystery. One thing is certain; he is a "created being," and that of the most exalted type.

The Battle of the Culture

He was before his fall "**Anointed Cherub that Covereth.**" That is, he was the guardian or protector of the "Throne of God." He was perfect in all his ways from the day that he was created, until iniquity was found in him. In him was the "fullness of wisdom," and the "perfection of beauty," but it was his "beauty" that caused the pride that was his downfall. He was clothed in a garment that was covered with the most rare and precious gems, the Sardis, topaz, diamond, beryl, onyx, jasper, sapphire, emerald, carbuncle, all woven in with gold. He dwelt in Eden the "Garden of God." This probably refers not to the earthly Eden, but to the "Paradise of God" on high, for Satan dwelt on the "Holy Mount of God." All this we learn from Ezek. 28:11-19, where the Prophet here describes Satan's original glory from which he fell. There never has been as yet such a King of Tyrus as is here described. The cause of Satan's fall is given in Isa. 14:12-20. He is there called—**Lucifer, Son of the Morning.** This was his glorious title when he was created, and this world of ours was made, at which time— "The Morning Stars, (probably other glorious created ruling beings like himself), sang together, and all the Sons of God,' (angels), shouted for joy." Job 38:7. It is well to note that the one here called "Lucifer, Son of the Morning," is in verse 4, (Isa. 14:4), also called the "King of Babylon." As there never has been a King of Babylon like the one here described, the description must be that of a "future" King of Babylon. And as "Antichrist is to have for his Capital City Babylon rebuilt," this is probably a foreview by the Prophet of Antichrist, as indwelt by "Lucifer," or Satan," in that day when he shall be "king of Babylon." Some think that when this world was created and fit for habitation, Satan was placed in charge of it, and it was then, as Isaiah declares, that Satan said in his heart— "I will ascend into heaven, I will exalt my throne above the 'Stars of God' (other ruling powers); I will sit also upon the Mount of the Congregation, in the sides of the North. I will ascend above the heights of the clouds; I will be like **The Most High:** and that it was for this presumptuous act that the "Pre-Adamite World" became a chaos, and "without form and void," as described in   Gen. 1:2.

This would justify the claim of Satan that this world belongs to him, and that he had the right and power to transfer the "kingdoms of the world" to Christ, if He would only acknowledge Satan's supremacy. (Matt. 4:8, 9) And it accounts for the persistent battle Satan is waging against the **"Almighty"** to retain his possession of the earth.

II. His Present Location.

The common notion is that Satan and his angels are imprisoned in Hell. This is not true. The angels described in 2 Pet. 2:4, and Jude 6, as having left their "first estate," and being "reserved in every lasting chain under darkness," are not Satan's angels. They are a special class of angels whose sin caused the Flood. They are the "Spirits in Prison" of whom Peter speaks in 1Pet. 3:18-20. We read in the first and second chapters of Job that it was the custom in Job's day for the "Sons of God" (angels), to appear at stated times in the presence of God to give an account of their stewardship, and that Satan Always appeared with them. When the Lord said to Satan—"From where do you come?" Then Satan answered the Lord and said, "From roaming about on the earth and walking around on it." Job.1:7. 2; 2. Satan then was at liberty "on the earth," and had "access to God," and was "not cast out of Heaven" in Job's day' B.C. 2000. Milton in his book "Paradise Lost" describes Satan as having been cast out Heaven in the time of Adam and Eve, and bases his description on Rev. 12:7-12. But as the Book of Revelation is a prophecy of "Things to Come," and that were all "future" in the Apostle John's day, Satan had not been cast out of heaven up to that time, A.D. 96, and as he has not cast out since, he must be still at liberty in the heavenlies and on the earth.

III. His Kingdom. Satan is a King, and has a Kingdom. "If Satan cast out Satan he is divided against himself; how shall then his 'kingdom' stand." Matt. 12:24-30. "We wrestle not against flesh and blood, but against Principalities, against Powers, against the Rulers of the Darkness of the World (Age), against Spiritual Wickedness in High Places, (the Heavenlies)." Eph. 6:12. From this we see that his kingdom consist of "Principalities," "Powers," "Age Rulers of Darkness," and "Wicked Spirits in the Heavenlies." These "Principalities" are ruled by "Princes," who control certain nations of our earth, as in the days of Daniel the Prophet, when a heavenly messenger was sent to Daniel, but was hindered "three weeks" from him by the "Prince of the Kingdom of Persia," Satan's ruling "Prince of Persia," until Michael the Archangel came to his rescue. Dan. 10:10-14. The subjects of Satan's Kingdom are— **1.) Angels.** Not the angels that are kept not to their first estate and who are reserved in everlasting chains under darkness unto the Judgment of the Great Day, (Jude 6), but angels who are at the liberty, and are now with Satan in the heavenlies (Rev. 12:9), and who, with him, are to be cast into the "Lake of Fire" prepared for the Devil and his angels. Matt. 25:41. Rev. 20:10. **2.) Demons.** There is but one Devil. Where the world "devils" occurs in the New Testament we should substitute the word "demons." These demons are a race or order of "bodiless spirits," supposed by many to be the bodiless spirits of the inhabitants of the Pre-Adamite Earth, who seek to re-embody themselves by taking up their abode in human beings. This we know they can do under certain conditions. Demon possession was common in Christ's day. These demons are wicked, unclean, vicious, and have power to derange both mind and body. Matt. 12:22; 15:22; Luke 4:35; 8:26-36; 9:42. They are the "Familiar Spirits" and "Wizards" of the Old Testament and the "Seducing Spirits" of whom Paul warned Timothy. 1 Tim. 4:1. **3.) Unregenerate Human Beings.** All unregenerate human beings are the subjects of Satan. Jesus called the "Tares" the "Children of the Wicked One," (Matt. 13:38), and He told the Pharisaical Jews that their father was the Devil.

The Triune Devil

John 8:44. **IV. His Methods. 1.) He is the Deceiver of the World.** By the "World" is meant all those who belong to the "Satanic System." All those who are entangled in Satan's mesh, "And we know that we are God, and the whole World (the Satanic System) lies in the power of the evil one, (Devil)." 1 John 5:19. Satan deceives by "blinding" the eyes of the world. "If our Gospel is hid, it is hid to them that are lost in whom the God of this World (Satan), Hath blinded the minds of them which believe not, lest the light of the glorious Gospel of Christ, who is the image of God, should shine unto them." 2Cor.4:3, 4. To this end Satan has his preachers who preach "another gospel." Gal. 1:6-9. That gospel is the "doctrine of the devils." 1 Tim. 4:1. He is the instigator of "The Great Apostasy." Peter, speaking of the "latter times" says— "But false prophets also arose among the people, just as there will also be false teachers among you, who will secretly introduce destructive heresies, even denying the Master who bought them, bringing swift destruction upon themselves. Many will follow their sensuality, and because of them the way of the truth will maligned; 2 Pet. 2:1, 2. These "false teachers" are to be seen on every hand. They are those who deny the "Virgin Birth," "Deity," "Bodily Resurrection" and "Personal Pre-millennial Return" of the Lord Jesus Christ. Satan is very subtle in his methods, and if it were possible he would deceive the very elect. He knows all the great scripture subjects that are of universal interest to humanity, and he is too wise to attack them openly, so he adulterates them with false doctrine. He has tried to rob the Church of her "Blessed Hope" of the Lord's return, by mixing with it a lot of false teaching and "time setting" as seen in "Seventh Day Adventism" and Millennial Darwinism." To prevent mankind from turning to the Lord for healing, he has invented the systems of "Christian Science" and "Scientology etc." To satisfy the craving of human mind to know what is going on in the Spirit World, Satan invented "Spiritualism." And when interest in it began to wane he revived it under the name of "Psychical Research." This system has existed from the earliest ages and has the unqualified condemnation of the Scriptures.

The Battle of the Culture

"There shall not be found among you anyone who makes his son or his daughter pass through the fire, one who uses divination, one who practices witchcraft, or one who interprets omens or a sorcerer, or one who casts spell, or a medium, or a spiritist, or one who calls up the dead. For whoever does these things is detestable to the Lord; and because of these detestable things the Lord your God will drive them out before you." Deu. 18:10-12. Spiritualism is only another name for "Demonism," and all professed impersonations are either counterfeit, or demonic. Christian Science teaches that there is such as "Malicious Animal Magnetism" by which one person may afflict another. It is only another name for "Diabolism." Those who dabble in "Spiritualism" or "Psychical Research," are liable to have their understanding darkened and come under the manipulation power of demons. Satan seeing that he could not stamp out the Church by violence and persecution has changed his tactics and is now trying to seduce her into conformity to the world and to try to better an "Age" that God has doomed to destruction. His present purpose is to build up a magnificent civilization and he has deceived the Church into believing that it can bring in the "Millennium," without Christ, by the **"Betterment of Society."** His hope is that the Gospel of Social Service will take the place of the "Gospel of Grace," and by diverting the attention of Christian people to secondary things, they will neglect the primary work of soul saving and thus delay the evangelization of the world and postpone the Return of the Lord, and his own confinement in the bottomless Pit. **2.) He is the Adversary of God's People,** the warfare (The Battle of the Culture) between "Good" and "Evil," as recorded in the Bible from Gen. 3:15 to Rev. 20:10, is most intensely interesting reading. Satan tempts Eve. She eats and Adam with her. They both are cast out of the Garden, first victory scored by Satan, Satan enters Cain, the result Abel is murdered. Victory number two for Satan, the "Sons of God" at Satan's instigation marry the "daughters of men," result the Flood. Victory number three for Satan, Noah delivered from the Flood is tempted to drink, yields, and a curse falls on Ham. Victories number four for Satan.

The Triune Devil

The people multiply and Satan fills their hearts with pride and presumption, the Tower of Babel is built, the result the "Confusion of Tongues," and the unity of the race broken up. Victories number five for Satan. Then God calls Abraham through whom the promised "Seed of the Woman," the Second Adam, should come who was to bruise Satan's head. Now the fight begins in earnest. We have only space to indicate it. First Satan closes Sarah's womb. Then when Isaac is born he seeks to have him slain by his father's hand on Mt. Moriah. He makes enmity between Esau and Jacob, hoping that the tragedy of Cain and Abel would be repeated. Then he causes Potiphar's wife to tempt Joseph, seeking to get him out the way. When the time came for Moses, the deliverer of the Children of Israel, to be born, he puts it in the heart of Pharaoh to order that all male Hebrew children shall be destroyed at birth. But the story is too long. The sin of David was Satan's work, and at one time the "royal seed" was narrowed down to one child. 2 Chron. 2:4-17, 10-12. When the time came that Christ was born, it was Satan who prompted Herod to destroy all the male children at Bethlehem less than two years of age. It was Satan who tried to overcome Christ when weakened by fasting in the Wilderness, and who suggested that Christ throw Himself down from the Pinnacle of the Temple. The attempt of the people to throw Him from the hilltop at Nazareth, and the two storms on Galilee were all attempts of Satan to destroy Christ. And when foiled in these Satan renewed the fight through Priests and Pharisees, and succeeded at last in getting Judas to sell his Master. Then amid the shades of Gethsemane he sought to kill Christ by physical weakness before He could reach the Cross. When Christ was crucified Satan thought he had conquered, but when Christ rose from the dead Satan's rage knew no bounds. In all probability Satan and his angels contested the Ascension of Christ, and the history of the Christian Church is but one long story of the "Irrepressible Conflict" between Satan and God's people.

The Battle of the Culture

Paul writing to the Thessalonians said: "For we wanted to come to you, I, Paul more than once and yet Satan hindered us. 1 Thess. 2:18. Even Paul's "thorn in the flesh" was the "Messenger of Satan" to buffet him. **V. His Expulsion From the Heavenlies.** As we have seen Satan still has his abode in the "Heavenlies" and has access to God. But the time is coming when he shall be cast out of the Heavenlies. It is described in Rev. 12:7-17. And there was war in Heaven. Michael and his angels fought against the Dragon, and the Dragon fought and his angels, and prevailed not; neither was their place found anymore in Heaven. And the Great Dragon was cast, that old "Serpent," called the "Devil," and "Satan," which deceived the whole world: he was cast out into the Earth and his angels were cast out with him. And I heard a loud voice saying in Heaven, now is come is come Salvation and Strength and the Kingdom of God, and the Power of His Christ; for the Accuser of Our Brethren Is Cast Down, which accused them before our God day and night." While Satan has been the "Accuser of the Brethren" in all Ages, the context shows that reference is here made to the "Jewish Remnant," (the brethren of Christ), who during the first three and one-half years of the "Tribulation Period" (for Satan is cast out in the Middle of the "Last Week," or Tribulation Period), pass through great persecution, and die as "martyrs." They are referred to in Rev. 6:9-11 as the "souls of them that were slain for the "Word of God," and we are here told (Rev. 12:11) that they overcame by the "Blood of the Lamb," and the "word of their testimony," and died as "martyrs," for they "loved not their lives unto the death." As they overcame by the "Blood of the Lamb," then the time of their overcoming must be subsequent to the shedding of Christ's blood on Calvary that is, Satan, according to this account, could not have been cast out of the "Heavenlies" prior to the Crucifixion of Christ. When Jesus said— "I beheld Satan as lightning fall from heaven," (Luke 10: 18), He was not referring to some past fall of Satan, but it was a prophetic utterance, by way of anticipation, of his future fall, when he shall be cast out of Heaven by Michael the Archangel.

The Triune Devil

As further evidence as to the "Time" of Satan's casting out, Daniel the Prophet tells us that it will be at the "Time of Trouble," (The Great Tribulation), that is to come upon Daniel's people, the Jews, for it is at that time that Michael the Great Prince is to stand up and they shall be delivered. Dan 12:1. As still further evidence that the casting out of Satan did not happen before the fall in Eden, we are told that it follows the birth and catching out the "Man Child," (Christ), (Rev. 12:5), that the earth shall be full of inhabitants, that is, thickly population, and that Satan shall be full of wrath, because he knows that he has but a "short time" (3 1/2 years), in which to finish his devilish work (Rev.12:12) **VI. His Incarnation,** When Satan is cast out the Heavenlies on to the earth, he is going to "incarnate" himself in the Antichrist. But the story is too long. The sin of David was Satan's work, and at one time the "royal seed" was narrowed down to one child. 2 Chron. 2:4-17, 10-12. When the time came that Christ was born, it was Satan who prompted Herod to destroy all the male children at Bethlehem under two years of age. It was Satan who tried to overcome Christ when weakened by fasting in the Wilderness, and who suggested that Christ throw Himself down from the Pinnacle of the Temple. The attempt of the people to throw Him from the hilltop at Nazareth, and the two storms on Galilee were all attempts of Satan to destroy Christ. And when foiled in these Satan renewed the fight through Priests and Pharisees, and succeeded at last in getting Judas to sell his Master. Then amid the shades of Gethsemane he sought to kill Christ by physical weakness before He could reach the Cross. When Christ was crucified Satan thought he had conquered, but when Christ was crucified Satan thought he had conquered, but when Christ rose from the dead Satan's rage knew no bounds. In all probability Satan and his angels contested the Ascension of Christ, and the history of the Christian Church is but one long story of the "Irrepressible Conflict" between Satan and God's people. Paul writing to the Thessalonians said: "For we wanted to come to you, I, Paul more than once and yet Satan hindered us.

The Battle of the Culture

1 Thess. 2:18. Even Paul's "thorn in the flesh" was the "Messenger of Satan" to buffet him. **V. His Expulsion From the Heavenlies.** As we have seen Satan still has his abode in the "Heavenlies" and has access to God. But the time is coming when he shall be cast out of the Heavenlies. It is described in Rev. 12:7-17. And there was war in Heaven. Michael and his angels fought against the Dragon, and the Dragon fought and his angels, and prevailed not; neither was their place found anymore in Heaven. And the Great Dragon was cast, that old "Serpent," called the "Devil," and "Satan," which deceived the whole world: he was cast out into the Earth and his angels were cast out with him. And I heard a loud voice saying in Heaven, now is come is come Salvation and Strength and the Kingdom of God, and the Power of His Christ; for the Accuser of Our Brethren Is Cast Down, which accused them before our God day and night." While Satan has been the "Accuser of the Brethren" in all Ages, the context shows that reference is here made to the "Jewish Remnant," (the brethren of Christ), who during the first three and one-half years of the "Tribulation Period" (for Satan is cast out in the Middle of the "Last Week," or Tribulation Period), pass through great persecution, and die as "martyrs." They are referred to in Rev. 6:9-11 as the "souls of them that were slain for the "Word of God," and we are here told (Rev. 12:11) that they overcame by the "Blood of the Lamb," and the "word of their testimony," and died as "martyrs," for they "loved not their lives unto the death." As they overcame by the "Blood of the Lamb," then the time of their overcoming must be subsequent to the shedding of Christ's blood on Calvary that is, Satan, according to this account, could not have been cast out of the "Heavenlies" prior to the Crucifixion of Christ. When Jesus said— "I beheld Satan as lightning fall from heaven," (Luke 10: 18), He was not referring to some past fall of Satan, but it was a prophetic utterance, by way of anticipation, of his future fall, when he shall be cast out of Heaven by Michael the Archangel. As further evidence as to the "Time" of Satan's casting out,

The Triune Devil

Daniel the Prophet tells us that it will be at the "Time of Trouble," (The Great Tribulation), that is to come upon Daniel's people, the Jews, for it is at that time that Michael the Great Prince is to stand up and they shall be delivered. Dan 12:1. As still further evidence that the casting out of Satan did not happen before the fall in Eden, we are told that it follows the birth and catching out the "Man Child," (Christ), (Rev. 12:5), that the earth shall be full of inhabitants, that is, thickly population, and that Satan shall be full of wrath, because he knows that he has but a "short time" (3 1/2 years), in which to finish his devilish work (Rev.12:12) **VI. His Incarnation,** When Satan is cast out the Heavenlies on to the earth, he is going to "incarnate" himself in the Antichrist.

VII. His Doom

When Christ shall return to the Mt. of Olives at the close of the "Tribulation Period," the "Beast" and the "False Prophet" shall be cast alive into the "Lake of Fire," and an angel from Heaven will seize Satan and bind him with a great chain, already forged, and cast him into the "Bottomless Pit," where he shall remain for 1000 years. Rev. 20, 1-3. At the close of which time he shall be loosed for a season, and then with his angels, demons and the human beings who have fallen under his power, he shall be cast into the "Lake of Fire" prepared for him. Rev. 20:7-10; Matt. 25:41. **THE ANTICHRIST,** In our study of prophecy we lay much stress on the "Second Coming of Christ," forgetting that there are two other comings of individuals that are just as momentous as Christ's coming. The first is that of Antichrist, and the other is of Satan. In both the Old and New Testament we are told are told a Mysterious and Terrible Personage that shall be revealed in the "Last times." He is described under different names and aliases, and it is only by a careful examination and comparison of these names, and the person they describe that we see that they refer to one and the same individual.

These names are— **In the Old Testament...Isaiah, 14:4— "King of Babylon." 14:12— "Lucifer." Daniel.7:8, 8:9— "The Little Horn." 8:23— "A King of Fierce Countenance." 9:26, "The Prince that Shall Come." 11:36, "The Willful King." In the New Testament. . .Paul 2 Thess. 2:3-8 "The Man of Sin" "Son of Perdition" "That Wicked." John...1 John 2:18— "Antichrist." Rev.13:1— "The Beast."** Jesus also made a prophetic reference to him. **I. His Personality.** The Apostolic Church believed that the Antichrist was to be a person the embodiment of human blasphemy and wickedness, but toward the close of the Twelfth Century many began to look upon the Pope as Antichrist, and this view has been largely advocated by Protestant commentators. The arguments in favor of this view are ingenious and plausible, but they are hard to reconcile with the Word of God. This view makes Antichrist a "System" rather than a person, and would see in the "Papal System" the Antichrist. But this is disproved by the Word of God. **1.)** The Apostle John says— "Who is a liar, but he that denied that Jesus is the Christ? He is Antichrist that denied the father and the Son." 1 John 2:22. "Every spirit that confessed not that Jesus Christ is come in the Flesh (his Deity) is not of God; and this is that spirit of Antichrist." 1 John 4:3. Judaism has denied that "Jesus is the Christ," and Unitarianism that He has come in the flesh but the Papacy never. The Church of Rome has always confessed— "I believe in God the Father Almighty, maker of heaven and earth, and Jesus Christ, His only Son, our Lord." **2.)** All Protestant commentators insist that the "Papal System" is described in Rev. 17:4, 5, under the figure of a "Woman" arrayed in purple and scarlet colors and deck with gold and precious stones and pearls.

The Triune Devil

This is undoubtedly true, but this "Woman, "the Mother of Harlots is represented as riding upon a Beast universally admitted to be the Antichrist. If the Beast is the Antichrist, the "Woman" cannot be and that they are separate and do not signify the same thing is clear. **3.)** Again Antichrist, as the "Man of Sin" is to— "Exalt himself and magnify himself above every god." Dan. 11:36, 37. "So that he as God sits in the Temple of God showing himself that he is God." 2 Thess. 2:4. However false and impious the claims of the Papacy, it always recognizes its subordination to God, and the Pope's highest claim is that he is the "Vicar of Christ." **4.)** "All the world wondered after the Beast (the Antichrist), and they worshipped the Dragon (the Devil), which gave power unto the Beast." Rev. 13:3, 4. The "Papal System" worships the "Virgin" and the "Saints," but it is not true that it worships the Devil. **5.)** "If any man worship the Beast and His Image, and receive his mark in his forehead, or in his hand, the same shall drink of the wine of the Wrath of God, ...and he shall be torment with fire and brimstone,....and the smoke of their torment ascended up forever and ever; and they have no rest day nor night, who worship the Beast and His Image and whosoever received the mark of his name. Rev.14:9-11.

If the "Papal System" is the Antichrist, it follows from the above that all its worshipers, instead of being saved, are doomed to eternal torment. Again, the Lord, who destroys Antichrist at His Coming, comes to Jerusalem, not to Rome, the seat of the "Papal System." While there are many things in the history of the Church of Rome, and in the conduct of her Popes that foreshadow the Antichrist, yet it is clear from the preceding scriptures can only be fulfilled in the person of some "Individual" yet to appear.

The Battle of the Culture

Antichrist is not a "Rival or "Counterfeit" Christ, he is an "Opposing" Christ. This is clearly seen when we compare him with Christ in a series of— Contrasts,

1.) Christ came from Above. John 6:38

   Antichrist ascends from the Pit. Rev. 11:7.

2.) Christ came in His Father's name. John 5:43.

   Antichrist comes in his own name. John 5:43.

3.) Christ Humbled Himself. Phil. 2:8.

   Antichrist Exalts himself. 2 Thess. 2:4.

4.) Christ Despised. Isa. 53:3; Luke 23:18.

   Antichrist Admired. Rev. 13:3, 4.

5.) Christ Exalted. Phil. 2:9.

   Antichrist Cast Down to Hell. Isa. 14:14, 15; Rev. 19:20.

6.) Christ to do His Father's will. John 6:36.

   Antichrist to do his Own will. Dan. 11:36.

7.) Christ came to Save. Luke 19:10.

   Antichrist comes to Destroy. Dan. 8:24

8.) Christ is the Good Shepherd. John 10:4-15.

   Antichrist is the Idol (evil) Shepherd. Zech 11:16, 17

9.) Christ is the "True Vine." John 15:1.

   Antichrist is the "Vine of the Earth." Rev.14:18.

10.) **Christ is the "Truth." John 14:6.**

   Antichrist is the "Lie" 2 Thess. 2:11,

11.) **Christ is the "Holy One." Mark 1:24.**

   Antichrist is the "Lawless One." 2 Thess. 2:8,

12.) **Christ is the "Man of Sorrows." Isa. 53:3.**

   Antichrist is the "Man of Sin." 2 Thess. 2:3.

13.) **Christ is the "Son of God." Luke 1:35.**

   Antichrist is the "Son of Perdition." 2 Thess. 2:3.

14.) **Christ, "The Mystery of Godliness," is God manifest in the flesh 1 Tim. 3:16.**

Antichrist, "The Mystery of Iniquity," will be Satan manifest in the flesh. 2 Thess. 2:7.

II. His Origin.

1.) **Isaiah's Foreview.** In Isa. 11:4— a chapter which is evidently Messianic—we read that among other things which the Messiah will do— "He shall smite the earth with the rod of His mouth and with the breath of His lips shall He slay The wicked." The word translated "The Wicked," is in the singular number, and cannot refer to wicked persons in general, but to some one person who is conspicuously wicked. The expression is strikingly like that of Paul's in 2 Thess. 2:8— "Then shall the Wicked be revealed, whom the Lord shall consume with the Spirit of His Mouth, and shall destroy with the "Brightness of His Coming."

The Battle of the Culture

It is evident that Isaiah and Paul refer to the same individual, who can be no other than the Antichrist. In Isa. 4-17 there is a description of a "King of Babylon" who shall smite the people in his wrath, and rule the nations in anger, and shall in his pride say— "I will ascend into heaven, I will exalt my throne above the Stars of God (Heavenly Rulers). I will sit also upon the mount of the congregation, in the sides of the north; I will ascend above the heights the clouds; I will be like the Most High." The king is called Lucifer, Son of the Morning, and his fall is described. He is cast down to Hell (Sheol, the Grave or Underworld), where his coming creates a great stir among the kings of the earth that have preceded him, and who exclaim when they see him— Even you have been made weak as we, you have become like us.......Is this the man who made the earth tremble, Who shook kingdoms, Which made the world like a wilderness and overthrow its cities, Who did not allow his prisoners to go home?" There has never as yet been such a king of Babylon as is here described. It must therefore refer to some future ruler of Babylon when Babylon shall be rebuilt, as it is to be. Verses 12 to 14 evidently refer to Satan and descriptive of him before his fall, but as he is to incarnate himself in the Antichrist, who is to be a future King of Babylon, it explains the source of the pride and presumption of Antichrist, which will lead to his downfall, as it did to Satan's. **2. Daniel's Foreview.** In the chapter on "The Gentiles" we described how Daniel saw come up among the "Ten Horns" on the head of the Fourth Wild Beast a "Little Horn," and this "Little Horn" had eyes like the eyes of a man, and a mouth speaking great things." Dan.7:7, 8. Daniel was told that this "Little Horn" was a king that should arise, and that he would be a person of remarkable intelligence and great oratorical powers, having a mouth speaking great things.

The Triune Devil

That he would be audacious, arrogant, imperious and persecuting, and change times and laws and that the Saints of the Most High (Daniel's own people the Jews) would be given into his hands for a "Time" and "Times" and the dividing of time, or 3 1/2 years. Dan. 7:23-26. Later Daniel had a vision of a Ram and a He-Goat contesting for supremacy. Dan. 8:1-27. The He-Goat had a notable horn between his eyes. This "Great Horn" was broken, and in its place four notable horns sprang up and out of one of them sprang forth a "Little Horn" which waxed exceedingly great toward the south, and toward the east and toward the Pleasant Land (Palestine). And it waxed great, even to the Host of Heaven and it cast down some of the Host and of the Stars (angels) to the ground and stamped upon them. He (the little Horn) magnified himself even to the Prince of the Host (the Lord God, Joshua 5:13-15, 1 Sam. 17:45) and by Him (the Little Horn— Antichrist) the daily sacrifice was taken away and the place of his sanctuary (the Temple) was cast down. Dan. 8:9-11. When Daniel asked for the meaning of the vision he was told that the Ram stood for the Medo-Persian Kingdom and the He-Goat for the Grecian and that the "Four Horns" that came up in the place of the "Great Horn" stood for "Four Kings" and that the "Little Horn" that came up on one "Four Horn" stood for a King of "Fierce Countenance," who in the latter time of their kingdom (the Four Worldwide Kingdoms and not the four Kingdoms into which the Grecian Empire was divided for the time will be that when the transgressors are come to the full"), shall stand up. This King shall understand dark sentence and His power shall be mighty but not by his own power (Satan shall incarnate himself in him), and he shall destroy wonderfully and shall prosper and practice and shall destroy the mighty and Holy People (the Jews). And through his policy also he shall cause craft to prosper in his hand (no one shall be able to buy without the mark of the beast. Rev. 13:17), and he shall magnify himself in his heart (2 Thess. 2:3,4) and by peace shall destroy many; he shall also stand up against the Prince of Princes, but he shall be broken without hand. Dan. 8:23-25.

The Battle of the Culture

This clearly identifies the 'Little Horn" or "King of Fierce Countenance" which came out of one of the "Four Horns" that took the place of the "Notable Horn" on the head of the He-Goat as the Antichrist for Antiochus Epiphanes (B.C. 175-165) nor any other ruler of the past has ever stood up against Jesus the "Prince of Princes." Neither was Antiochus Epiphanes broken without hand he died a natural death at Tabae in B.C. 165. But the Antichrist is to be broken without hand. His Kingdom is to be destroyed by a stone cut out of the mountain without hands the "Stone Kingdom" of the Lord Jesus Christ, Dan. 2:34, 35, 44, 45 and he himself shall be paralyzed by the brightness of the Lord's Coming (1 Thess. 2:8), and be cast alive into the Lake of Fire. Rev. 19:20. Two good men, Enoch and Elijah, were translated to Heaven without dying and two bad men, spoken of officially as the Beast and the False Prophet shall be cast into the lake of Fire without dying. Those who claim that the "Little Horn" of Dan.7, and the "Little Horn" of Dan.8 are not the same because the "Little Horn" of Dan.7 arises amid the "Ten Horns," of the Fourth Beast, which represents the Roman Empire and the "Little Horn" of Dan.8, arises on one of the Four Horns, that take the place of the "Great Horn" on the head of the He-Goat, which represents the Third Beast the Grecian Empire, forget that the vision that the Apostle John had of the revived Roman Empire (Rev. 13:1,2— the Roman Empire in its last stage), reveals the fact that the last stage of the Roman Empire will include all the characteristics of the whole Four Empire, Babylonian, Medo-Persian, Grecian and old Roman. This is seen in the character of the "Beast" John saw come up out of the sea. It was like unto a Leopard (Greece) reveals the fact that the preponderating feature of the revived Roman Empire will be Grecian and that therefore the "Ten Federated Kingdoms" will include the Four Kingdom into which the Grecian Empire was divided, Egypt, Macedon, Thrace, and Syria. It follows therefore that the "Little Horn" that arises on the "Fourth Horn" of the Fourth Beast (Rome).

The Triune Devil

Those who claim that the "little Horn" that came up on one of the Four Horns of the He-Goat was fulfilled in Antiochus Epiphanes (who was a king of Syria) overlook the fact that while Antiochus Epiphanes devastated Palestine and caused an idol altar to be erected on the altar of the Temple, on which he offered swine's flesh, which was an abomination to the Jews, he does not fulfill the description of the "Little Horn" of the He-Goat. Dan. 8:9-13. He does not compare with him for satanic malice. The "Abomination of Desolation" that Daniel refers to (Dan.9:27) is to occur in the last half of "Daniel's Seventieth Week" and as Jesus spoke of it as still unfulfilled in His day (Matt. 24:15), it is clear that Antiochus Epiphanes was not the fulfillment of the "Little Horn" of Dan.8:9-13. While it was revealed to Daniel that the "Little Horn" or Antichrist should come out of one of the "Four Horns that took the place of the "Great Horn" on the head of the He-Goat, he needed further light as to which one. We now know from history that the "Great Horn" represented Alexander the Great and that the "Four Notable Horns" that took the place of the Great Horn at the death of Alexander the Great represented the Four Kingdoms into which his kingdom was divided, visible, Egypt, Macedon, Thrace, and Syria, which included Assyria. These Four Kingdoms were in time all absorbed into the "Fourth World Kingdom," the Roman Empire, the last to lose its identity being Egypt, which succumbed in B.C. 30. That Daniel might know in which one of these Four Kingdoms the "Little Horn," or Antichrist, should arise, 15 years after his vision of the "Ram and He-Goat" the Lord gave him a third vision, that of two kings, the "King of the North" and the "King of the South." Dan. 11:1-45. The "King of the North" was the King of Syria, and as his character and conduct described (Dan.11:36-38) as similar to that of the "Little Horn" that came out of one the "Four Horns" it is clear that the Antichrist is to come from Syria. That the "King of the North" spoken of in Dan. 11:21-31 was Antiochus Epiphanes there can be no question, but that he was not the "Little Horn," or the Antichrist, who is to come out of Syria in the "latter days" is clear from the remainder of the chapter from the 35th verse, which describes the conduct of the future Antichrist.

The Battle of the Culture

The intervening verse, the 32nd to the 35th inclusive, fills in the gap between the time of Antiochus Epiphanes and the appearance of the Antichrist. There is no intimation that Antiochus Epiphanes is even to be regarded as a type of Antichrist. They are distinct historical personages each dealt with in his own place, and though they resemble each other in some respects yet must not be confounded with each other. The terms "North" and "South" are applied to Syria and Egypt because of their geographic relation to Palestine (the Pleasant) or Glorious Land. Dan. 8:9; 11:16, 41). In the thought of Jehovah Jerusalem is at once the geographic and moral centre of the earth. We are to understand therefore by the "King of the North" the King of Syria, which also included Assyria. This fixes the locality from which the Antichrist shall come, for we read in Isa. 10:12— "So it will be that when the Lord has completed all His work on Mount Zion and on Jerusalem, He will say, "I will punish the fruit of the arrogant heart of the King of Assyria and the pomp of his haughtiness." and we read in Isa. 14:25— "I will stand to break Assyria in my land, and I will trample him on My Mountains. Then his yoke will be removed from them and his burden removed from them and his burden removed from their shoulder." The context shows that this prophecy is connected with the restoration of Israel to their land and the time of the downfall of Antichrist. To recapitulate, we see from the three visions of Daniel that— 1.) He learned from the "Little Horn" of the Fourth Wild Beast, that a Mysterious and Terrible Personage was to arise in the "Latter Days." 2.) He learned from the "Little Horn" of the "Great Horn" on the He-Goat, that. that "Terrible Personage" was to come out of one of the Kingdoms into which the Grecian Empire was divided at the death of Alexander the Great. 3.) He learned the vision of the "King of the North" that "Terrible Personage" would come out the Syrian division of Alexander's Kingdom. The Antichrist, therefore, in all probability will be a Syrian Jew, for it is not likely that the Jews will accept as the Messiah one who is not a Jew, unless the claimant by false pretence makes them believe he is one.

This, however, does not prevent the Antichrist being a Roman citizen, and a King of the revived Roman Empire, for Saul of Tarsus was both a Jew and a Roman citizen. **3.) Paul's Foreview.** Writing to the Thessalonians, Paul says— "Let no man deceive you by any means; for that day (the Day of the Lord) shall not come except there come a falling away first and that Man of Sin be revealed, the Son of Perdition who opposed and exalted himself above all that is called God, or that is worshipped; so that he As God sits in the Temple of God (the rebuilt Temple at Jerusalem), showing himself that he is God......For the Mystery of Iniquity doth already work (in Paul's day); only He (the Holy Spirit) who now will let (restrain), until He be taken out of the way. And then shall That Wicked be revealed whom the Lord shall consume with the spirit (breath) of His mouth and shall destroy with the brightness (manifestation) of His Coming. Even him, whose coming is after the working of Satan with all power and signs and lying wonders and with all deceivableness of unrighteousness in them that perish; because they received not the love of the truth, that they might be saved." 2 Thess. 2:3-10. In the New American Standard Edition of the Bible, the Antichrist is called the "Mystery of Lawlessness" or the "Lawless One." As such he is not the cause of "Lawlessness," he is the result or fruit of it, for he will arise out of the seething cauldron of "Lawlessness" that is now becoming pronounced and manifest the world. The name that the Apostle Paul gives the Antichrist, the— "Son of Perdition," is not without significance. The name is used but twice in the Scripture. It is first used by Christ of Judas (John 17:12), and then here of Antichrist. The Apostle also calls the Antichrist in this passage the "Mystery of Iniquity." What does that mean? In 1 Tim. 3:16, Christ is spoken of as the "Mystery of Godliness." That is, that He was God Manifest in the Flesh. How did He manifest in the flesh? By being born of the Virgin Mary by the Holy Spirit, Thus it was that Jesus became the "Son of God." Luke 1:35. Now as iniquity is the opposite of Godliness, then the "Mystery of Iniquity" must be the opposite of the "Mystery of Godliness."

The Battle of the Culture

That is, if Christ is the "Mystery of Godliness," Antichrist must be the "Mystery of Iniquity," and as Christ was the "Son of God," then Antichrist must be the "Son of Perdition," that is Satan. And as Christ was born of a virgin by the Holy Spirit, so Antichrist will be born of a Woman (not necessarily a virgin) by Satan. This is no new view for it has been held by many of God's spiritually minded children since the days of the Apostle John, and there is some warrant for it in the Scriptures. In Gen. 3:15, God said to the Serpent (Satan), I will put enmity between thee and the woman, and between "Thy Seed and Her Seed." Now the woman's Seed was Christ, then the Serpent's Seed must be Antichrist. In John 8:44 Jesus said to the Jews— "You are of your father the devil, and you want to do the desires of your father. He was a murderer from the beginning, and does not stand in the truth because there is no truth in him. Whenever he speaks a lie, he speaks from his own nature, for he is a liar and the father of lies. In the Greek there is the definite article before "lie" and it should read "The Lie," so when the Devil speaks of The Lie he is speaking of his own (child), for he is liar, and the Father of "It" — "The Lie." And it is worthy of note that in the verse (vs11) that follows the passage we are considering that the Apostle says— " And for this cause God shall send them strong delusion that they should believe a lie." Here again the definite article is found in the Greek, and it should read "The Lie," the "Son of Perdition," the Antichrist. But why was Judas called the "Son of Perdition"? Was he a child of Satan by some woman, or was he simply indwelt by Satan? Here we must let the Scriptures speak for themselves. In John 6:70-71 we read that Jesus said "Have not I chosen you twelve, and one of you is a Devil? He spake of Judas Iscariot the son of Simon; for him, it was that he should betray Him, being one of the Twelve." In no other passage than this is the word "Devil" applied to anyone but Satan himself. Here the Greek word is "diabolus" the definite article is employed and it should read— "and one of you is "The Devil" This would make Judas the Devil incarnated, or the "Mystery of Iniquity," and explains why Jesus in John 17:12, calls him the "Son of Perdition."

The Triune Devil

This is the only place in Scriptures where the word "diabolus," the is applied to a human being and implies an incarnation. While "Perdition" is a place (Rev.17:8, 11), it is also a condition into which men may fall (1 Tim. 6:9; Heb. 10:39), and while men who have committed the "Unpardonable Sin" are sons of perdition, because they are destined to the place of the irrevocably lost, yet Judas and Antichrist are the "Sons of Perdition" in a special sense, for they are sons of the author of Perdition— The Devil. That is they are not merely "obsessed" or controlled by the Devil, the Devil has incarnated himself in them, and for the time being, to all practical purposes, they are the very Devil himself. The next question that arises is if Judas and the Antichrist are both called the Son of Perdition, are they one and the same, or are there two Sons of Perdition? Here we must anticipate. Turning to Rev.11:7, we read that the beast that slays the two Witnesses ascends out of the "Bottomless Pit" (Abyss), and that Beast is the Antichrist. Now how did he get into the Abyss? Well, if there is only one Son of Perdition, and Judas and Antichrist are one and the same, and then he got in the Abyss when Judas went to his "Own Place" (the Abyss). Acts.1:25. Of no other person is it said anywhere in the Scriptures that he went "to his own Place." Again in Rev. 17:8 it is said— "The Beast that you saw was, and is not, and is about to come up out of the abyss and go to destruction (Perdition)." As this Beast is the same that slays the Two Witness he is the Antichrist. Now there are four things said of him. 1.) He "Was," 2.) He "Is Not," 3.) He "Shall Ascend out of the Bottomless Pit," 4.) He shall "Go into Perdition." From this we learn that in John's the Beast was not but that he had been before on the earth, and was to come again, that he was to Ascend from the bottomless pit. This is positive proof that the Antichrist has been on the earth before and that when he comes in the future he will come from the "Abyss." The question then arises, when was "Antichrist" on the earth before? If Judas and Antichrist are one and the same the enigma is solved.

The Battle of the Culture

When Judas was on earth, he was; when Judas went to his "Own place" he "Was Not"; when Judas comes back from the "Abyss" he will be— The Antichrist. The Author does not insist on the view of Judas and the Antichrist being correct, but with open mind he accepts it, because it seems to be the only logical solution of both Judas and Antichrist being called the "Son of Perdition." **4.) John's Foreview.** On the Isle of Patmos the Apostle John had his vision of the Antichrist. "And I stood upon the sand of the sea, and saw a Beast rise up out of the sea (Mediterranean Sea), having Seven Heads and Ten Horns and upon his heads the name of blasphemy. And the Beast which I saw was like unto a Leopard, and his feet were as the feet of a Bear, and his mouth as the mouth of a Lion; and The Dragon gave him his power, and seat, and great authority. And I saw one of his heads as it were wounded to death; and his deadly wound was healed; and all the world wondered after The Beast and they worshipped The Dragon which gave power unto the Beast; and they worshipped The Beast saying, Who is like unto the Beast? Who is able to make war with him? And there was given unto him a mouth speaking Great Things and Blasphemies and power was given unto him to continue forty and Two Months. And he opened his mouth In Blasphemy against God, to Blaspheme His Name, and His Tabernacle and Them That Dwell in Heaven. And it was given unto him to make War with the Saints (not the saints of the Church; they were already in glory) and to overcome them; and Power Was Given Him over All Kindred and Tongues and Nations. And all that dwell upon the earth shall worship him, whose names are written in the Book of Life of the Lamb slain from the foundation of the world." Rev.13:1-8. When we compare these "Foreviews," and note the similarity of conduct of Daniel's "Little Horn," Paul's Man of Sin, and John's Beast are to continue for the same length of time— "Forty and Two Months," or 31/2 years, and that Daniel's "Little Horn," Paul's "Man of Sin," and John's "Beast," are all to be destroyed in the same "Evil Power" which is after the "Working of Satan," and which John in 1 John 2:18, calls The Antichrist.

The Triune Devil

In other words when we find in prophecy three Symbolic Personages" that come upon the stage of action at the same time work, exist the same length of time, and meet the same fate; they must symbolize the Same Thing. Before we examine in detail John's Beast, it would be well for us to compare it with Daniel's "Fourth Wild Beast." In comparing these two "Beasts" we find that they both come up out of the sea (the nations), and that they are utterly unlike any beast we have ever heard of. Daniel's "Beast" was dreadful and terrible, and strong exceedingly; and it had great iron teeth and nails of brass; while John's Beast was like a Leopard, with the feet of a Bear, and the mouth of a Lion. As Daniel's "Beast" represented the "Fourth Kingdom" upon the earth, the Roman Empire, it is evident that its characteristics describe the old Roman Empire, while the characteristics of John's Beast represent the revived Roman Empire. We know that the Old Roman Empire was strong exceedingly and its grip and power were like a beast with great iron teeth and nails of brass and from the description of John's Beast we learn that the revived Roman Empire shall embody all the characteristics of the Four World Empires, as seen in its Leopard like body, its feet of a Bear, and its mouth of a Lion. That both "Beast" have Ten Horns" of Daniel's "Beast" stand for the same. Rev. 17:12. From this we see that both Daniel and John foresaw that the Roman Empire was to be eventually divided into "Ten Separate but Federated Kingdoms." While both "Beasts" have Ten Horns, they differ in that of John's who had "Seven Heads" while Daniels "Beast" had but one, and among the Ten Horns on Daniels "Beast" there came up a "Little Horn," which is not seen amid the 'Ten Horns" of John's Beast. These, as we shall see, are features that refer to the last stages of the Beast without carefully comparing Daniel's and John's "Beast," for the "Little Horns" of Daniel's "Beast" plucks up Three of the "Ten Horns" and destroys them, or takes their Kingdom away, a thing that John omits to tell us.

The Battle of the Culture

Again the Antichristian character of Daniel's "Beast" is seen in its "Little Horn" whose conduct corresponds with not a part, but the whole of John's "Beast," and that for the same length of time—"Time" and "Times" and the "Dividing of Time" which equals "Forty and Two Months." It now remains to analyze the "Beast" that John saw come up out of the sea, and tries to discover the meaning of its various members. We have two descriptions of this "Beast." Daniel's "Fourth Wild Beast" as we have seen, represents the Roman Empire as it existed from B.C. 30, until as a nation it shall cease to exit. While it was divided in A.D. 364, as the result of an ecclesiastical schism, into its Eastern and Western Divisions, and lost its national life as a world power, yet it has never lost its religious existence or influence as seen in the continuance of the Greek and Roman Churches, and Roman Law is still a controlling power in our laws. In this sense the Roman Empire in its influence has never ceased to exist. We are now to consider it in its last stage as out-lined in John's "Beast." In the descriptions of John's Beast as given it is very important to note that the "Beast" has a dual meaning. It represents both the revived Roman Empire, and its Imperial Head the Antichrist. As the revived Roman Empire it is seen coming up out of the sea of nations, as the Antichrist it comes up out of the Abyss. For instance it cannot be said of the Roman Empire of John's day, that it was, and Is Not, for it was at the height of its power in John's day. Neither can it be said of it that it shall ascend out of the pit and go into Perdition that could only be said of a person. Again we must distinguish between the body of the "Beast" and its heads and horns. The body being that of a Leopard, with the feet of a Bear, and the mouth of Lion is to show that the revived Roman Empire in its last stage will include the characteristics of the first Three Wild Beast of Daniel, that is, of the Lion (Babylon), the Bear (Medo-Persia), and the Leopard (Greece), and as the largest part of the "Beast," the body, is represented by the Leopard, the prevailing characteristic of the revived Roman Empire will be Grecian. The "Beast" that comes up out of the sea has seven heads and ten horns, and the Horns are crowned.

The Triune Devil

This represents the "Beast" or empire, at the height of its power, when it will have its entire "Heads," and when the Ten kings, the heads of the Ten kingdoms into which the Empire shall be divided, will have been crowned. The "beast" that comes up out the Abyss also has Seven Heads and Ten Horns, but they are not crowned, for the Ten Kings represented by the Ten Horns, have not as yet received their Kingdom. (Rev. 17:12.) This implies that the "Beast" of Rev. 17, represents the Antichrist at the beginning of the "Week." As confirmation of this view the "Woman," is seen at this stage riding the "Beast." For while the "Scarlet Clothed" is not seen until Chapter 17 it is clear that's she rides the "Beast" from the beginning of the "Week," for she represents the "Papal Church" that comes into power after the true church has been caught out. During the wars preceding the rise of the Antichrist the nations will be ten in number, represented by the "Ten Horns" of the "Beast." No doubt the "Papal Church" will play a prominent part in the proceedings. She will be rewarded by restoration to political power, and this union of the Church and State, in which the Church will have control, is shown by the woman riding the Beast, thus dominating it. But when the "Ten Kings" shall receive their Kingdoms and be crowned, they" shall hate the Whore, and shall make her desolate and naked, and shall eat her flesh, and burn her with fire." (vs.16). While we are told in Rev. 17:9 that the Seven Heads of the "Beast" represent "Seven Mountains" (this is to identify it with the Roman Empire), we are told in the next verse that they (the Seven Heads) also represent "Seven Kings" of whom "Five are fallen, and one is, and the other is not yet come; and when he comes he must continue a short space." That is, in John's day "Five" of these Kings had fallen, one was the ruling Emperor, and the "Seventh" was yet to come. **Who are meant by the first "Five Kings," that had fallen (Babylon, Persia, Greece, Egypt, Syria and a future turkey).** The King that was on the throne in John's day was Domitian, who had banished John to the Isle of Patmos. The last or "Seventh King" who is yet to come is undoubtedly the Antichrist. We are told in Rev. 13:3, that one of the "seven Heads," or "Kings" received a deadly wound.

The Battle of the Culture

Which one is not stated? The interference is that it is the, last for the Beast has all of his "Heads" before one of them is wounded. In Rev. 17:11 he is called the Beast that "Was" and "Is Not," even he is the "Eighth," and is of the "Seventh," and goes into Perdition. The only clear explanation of the passage is that the "Seventh Head"— The Antichrist, is the one who receives the deadly wound probably at the hand of an assassin , and as his body is lying in state prepared for burial, he rises from the dead (Rev. 13:14) and thus becomes the "Eighth" though he is of the "Seventh." By this resurrection of the Antichrist, Satan imitates the Resurrection of the Christ and makes the world wonder after the Beast (Rev. 13:3) and this adds to this prestige and power. If this happens at the "Middle of the Week," at the time the Dragon is cast out of Heaven, it will account for the great change that takes place in the Antichrist, for before receiving his "Deadly Wound" he will be sweet and lovable, but after his resurrection or recovery he becomes Devilish, the result of the Dragon incarnating himself in him. It is at the time he breaks the Covenant with the Jews and desecrates the Temple by setting up the "Abomination of Desolation" which is an "Idol Image" of himself— the "Desolator." As the "Little Horn' of Daniel's "Fourth Wild Beast" he will destroy three of the "Ten Kings" and firmly establish himself in the place of power, and as he, as the "Little Horn," does not appear until after the "Ten Horns," or "Ten Federated Kingdoms," come into existence, it is clear that the Antichrist does not form the Federation, but is the outgrowth of it.   III. His Character. He will be a composite man. One who embraces in his character the abilities and powers of Nebuchadnezzar, Xerxes, Alexander the Great and Caesar Augustus. He will have the marvelous gift of attracting unregenerate men, and the irresistible fascination of his personality, his versatile attainments, superhuman wisdom, great administrative and executive ability, along with his power as a consummate flatterer, a brilliant diplomatist, a superb strategist, will make him the most conspicuous and prominent of men.

The Triune Devil

All these gifts will be conferred on him by Satan, whose tool he will be, and who will thus make him the— **SUPERMAN,** He will pose as a great humanitarian, the friend of men, and the special friends of the Jewish race, whom he will persuade that he has come to usher in the "Golden Age" as pictured by the prophets, and who will receive him as Messiah. He will intoxicate men with a strong delusion and his never varying success. And when he shall be slain and rise again he will have lost none of these powers, but will be in addition the embodiment of all kinds of wickedness and blasphemy. "He shall speak great words against the Most High, and shall wear out the saints of the Most High, and think to change times and laws." Dan. 7:25. "He shall also stand up against the "Prince of Princes" (Jesus). Dan. 8:25. "He shall do according to his will; and he shall exalt him and magnify   himself above every god, and shall speak marvelous things against the God of Gods." Dan.11:36 "Who opposed and exalted himself above all that is called God, or that is worshipped; so that he as God sits in the Temple of God (at Jerusalem) showing himself that he Is God.... Whose coming is after the Working of Satan with all Power and Signs and lying Wonders?" 2 Thess. 2:3-9, there has never as yet appeared on this earth a person who answers the description given in the Scriptures. Such a character is almost inconceivable. No writer would have invented such a character. **IV. His Reign.** He shall reign for seven years, or during the whole of Daniel's "Seventieth Week." "And he shall confirm the Covenant with many for one week (Daniel's Seventieth week) and in the midst of the week he shall cause the sacrifice and oblation to cease." Dan. 9:27. After the Church has been caught out the Jews will be gathered back to their own land   unconverted. About this time ten of the Nations occupying the territory of the old Roman Empire will enter into a Federation. Among the Ten Kings of those nations will raise the Antichrist. He will soon prove himself to be a Great Ruler and will be made President. The Government will be a Democratic Monarchy. The President will make a "Covenant with the Jewish people, it may be a Covenant restoring to them their own land. Whatever its character, the Prophet Isaiah speaks of it as a "Covenant with Death and Hell." Isa. 28:15.

The Battle of the Culture

For 3 1/2 years the President of the Federation Kingdom will keep the Covenant, then he will break it for the balance of his 3 1/2 years, he will cause an awful persecution of the Jews, called "The Great Tribulation." It will not, however, be limited to them, for we read in Rev. 13:7, 8, that shall be given power "over all kindred's, and tongues and nations. And all that dwell upon the earth shall worship him, whose names are not written in the Book of Life."

V. His Doom. At the end of the seven years the allied armies of the Ten Federated Nations will gather together in the Valley of Megiddo, north of Jerusalem, to besiege that city. Zech. 14:2. The Lord will pour upon the "House of David" (Israel), and the inhabitants of Jerusalem, the "spirit of grace and supplication" (Zech. 12:10). Then the Lord, at the head of the armies of Heaven,' will come to their rescue (Rev. 19:11-16), and the Jews will see Christ descend upon Mt. of Olives (Zech.14:4) and the Beast (Antichrist) and the kings of the earth, and their armies will gather together to make war against the Lord, and the Beast and the False Prophet will be taken and cast alive into the "Lake of Fire" and the remnant of those armies shall be slain with the sword of Him who sits upon the "White Horse," and the fowls of the air will be summoned unto the "Supper of the Great God" and shall feed on the flesh of the kings, and captains, and of mighty men. Rev.19:17-21. **THE SATANIC TRINITY,** Satan is the "God of this World." (Age) 2 Cor. 4:4. As the God of this world, he aims to "ape" God. As God sent His Son (Jesus) into the world, so Satan shall send Antichrist into the world. As God was in Christ, so Satan will incarnate himself in Antichrist. The "Mystery of Godliness" is God manifest in the flesh. 2 Thess. 2:7. Satan will see to it that Antichrist has all that Christ has. **I.** Christ has a Church—the "Ecclesia" Antichrist will have a church, the synagogue of Satan. Rev.2:9; 3:9. **II.** Christ will have a Bride, the "Church," Eph.525-27; Antichrist will have a bride, the "Mystic Harlot Church." Rev.17:1-16. **III.** Christ has a Cup, "The Communion Cup," 1 Cor.10:16. 11:25; Antichrist has a cup, the "Cup of Devils" 1 Cor.10:21. **IV.**

The Triune Devil

Christ's earthly ministry lasted for three and a half years, and Satan shall reign in Antichrist for the same length of time. **V.** Christ died at the age thirty-three years, and for ought we know Antichrist shall be smitten at the same age; the age at which Alexander the Great, the "Great Horn" of the He-Goat, died. **VI.** The Godhead is a Trinity, Father, Son and Holy Spirit, and Satan proposes, as the "God of this Age," to manifest himself as a Trinity. In contradistinction to Divine Trinity we call this manifestation a **SATANIC TRINITY.,** The members of it are— 1 "The Dragon" the Anti-God. 2. "The Beast"— the "Anti-Christ." 3. "The False Prophet," the Anti-Spirit." We have spoken of the first two under the heads of Satan and Antichrist, all that we need to consider in chapter is— THE FALSE PROPHET., after the Apostle John had seen and described the "Beast" that came up out Sea, he saw another "Beast" come up out of the Earth. This "Second Beast," while John does not say it was a lambs, had "Two Horns" "like a lamb" that is, it was Lamb-Like because of this resemblance many claim that the "Second Beast" is the Antichrist, for Antichrist is supposed to imitate Christ. While the Lamb (Christ) is mentioned in the Book of Revelation 22 times, the description given of Him in Chapter 5:6, is that of a lamb having "Seven Horns" and not "Two." This differentiates Him from the lamb-like Beast that comes up out the earth, who though he is "lamb-like in appearance Speaks as a Dragon." The "Second Beast" has a name. He is called the "False Prophet" three times. In chapter 16:13, 19:20, 20:10, twice he is associated with the "First Beast," and as they are Persons so must he be. The fact that he called the "False Prophet" is proof that he is not the "Antichrist." Jesus had a foreview of him when He said— "There shall arise False Christ's and False Prophets and shall show Great signs and wonders insomuch that, if it were possible they shall deceive the very elect." Matt.24:24. Here Jesus differentiates between "False Christ's" and "False Prophets" therefore the "Antichrist" and the "False Prophet" cannot be the same. That the "Second Beast" comes up out of the Earth may signify that he will be a resurrected person.

The Battle of the Culture

If, as was hinted at, "Antichrist" was Judas resurrected, why should not the "False Prophet" also be a resurrected person? There will be two persons, as we have seen, who shall come back from Heaven as the "Two Witness," Moses and Elijah, why not two persons come up from "The Underworld," brought up by Satan to counteract the work of "Two Witness"? The fact that the "First Beast" (Antichrist) and the "Second Beast" (False Prophet) are cast Alive into the "Lake of Fire" (Rev. 19:20 is further proof that they are more than ordinary mortals, and that the "First Beast" is more than the last ruling Emperor of the revived Roman Empire. He is Antichrist, Satan's Superman. In the "Dragon," the "Beast," and the "False Prophet" we have the "Satanic Trinity," Satan's imitation of the "Divine Trinity." In the unseen and invisible "Dragon" we have the Father (the Ant-God). In the "Beast" we have the "Son of Perdition" (the Anti-Christ), begotten of the Dragon, who appears on the earth, dies, and is resurrected, and to whom is given a throne by his Father the Dragon. In the "False Prophet" we have the "Dragon Son," and whose speech is like the Dragon's. The "Dragon" then will be the "Anti-God" the "Beast" the "Anti-Christ," and the "False Prophet" the "Anti-Spirit," and the fact that all three are cast Alive into the "Lake of Fire" (Rev.20:10) is proof that they together form a "Triumvirate" which we may call—"The Satanic Trinity." Again the "Antichrist" is to be a King and rule over a Kingdom. He will accept the "Kingdoms of this world" that Satan offered Christ, and that Christ refused. Matt. 4:8-10. He will also exalt himself, and claim to be God.   2Thess.2:4. But the "False Prophet" is not a King, He does not exalt himself, he exalts the "First Beast" (Antichrist). His relation to the "First Beast" is the same as the Holy Spirit's relation to Christ. He caused the earth and them which dwell therein to worship the "First Beast." He also has power to give life, and in this he imitates the Holy Spirit. And as the followers of Christ are sealed by the Holy Spirit until the "Day of Redemption" (Eph. 4:30); so the followers of Antichrist shall be sealed by the False Prophet until the "Day of Perdition." Rev.13:16-17.

The Triune Devil

The False Prophet will be a "Miracle Worker." While Jesus will be of the Holy Spirit, Acts 10:38. Among the miracles that the False Prophet will perform he will bring down Fire from Heaven. As we have seen under the work of the "Two Witness," Rev.11:1-14, there will probably be a "Fire-Test" between Elijah and the False Prophet, and the test as to who is God of Mount Carmel will be repeated. That Satan, who will then energize the False Prophet, can do this is clear from Job1:16, where Satan, having secured per-mission from God to touch all that Job had, brought down "fire from heaven" and burned up Job's sheep and servants. The False Prophet then commands the people to make an "Image of the Beast" This is further proof that the "First Beast" is the Antichrist. It is a weakness of mankind that they must have some Visible God to worship, and when the Children of Israel, who had been delivered from Egypt under Moses leadership, thought he had forsaken them because he did not come down from the on Mount, they called Aaron to make them gods which should go before them, and Aaron made for them the "Golden Calf." Ex. 32:1-6. So the False Prophet will have the people make for the purpose of worship an "Image of the Beast." But the wonderful thing about the "Image" is that the False Prophet will have power to give Life to it, and cause it to Speak, and to demand that all who will not worship it shall be to death. In other words the "Image" will be a living, speaking, Automation. This "Image" reminds us of the "Golden Image" that Nebuchadnezzar commanded to be made and set up in the "Plain of Dura," in the Province of Babylon (Dan. 3:1-30), before which, at the sounding of musical instruments, the people were commanded to bow down and worship under penalty, for those who disobeyed, of being cast into a "Burning Fiery Furnace." Doubtless there will be many in the "Day of antichrist" who will refuse to blow down and worship the "Image of the Beast," and who will not escape as did the "Three Hebrew Children," though God may interpose in a miraculous way to deliver some. And as if this was not enough the False Prophet shall cause some.

The Battle of the Culture

And as if this was not enough the False Prophet shall cause—"All, both small and great, rich and poor, free and bond, to receive a Mark in their Right Hand or in their Forehead; and that no man might Buy or Sell save he that has the Mark or the Name of the Beast or the Number of His Name" this "Mark" will be known as the **"BRAND OF HELL."**

CHAPTER II

THE KINGDOM OF GOD VS THE KINGDOM OF DEVIL

THE PRESENT EVIL WORLD. while this is the "Dispensation of Grace," and God's purpose during it is to gather out a people for His name— the Church, the world out of which the Church is being gathered is called— "The Present Evil Age." Gal. 1:4. That this Age is Evil is seen in the character of its civilization. After nearly 2000 years of Gospel preaching the world is in a worse state, in proportion to its light than it was in the days Christ, and seems headed toward some great crisis. The spirit of lawlessness is in the air, and despite all efforts to quench it, it is strangely becoming unmanageable and perverse and determined to break away from all authority and law. How are we to account for this? Has God lost His control over the world, or is He permitting some other agency to have its way? **TWO OPPOSSING SPIRITS** at work in the world in this Dispensation. The "Holy Spirit" is engaged in gathering out the elect body of the Church and the spirit of Evil.

The Battle of the Culture

These are called in 1 Cor. 2:12. The "Spirit of God," "Spirit of the World," and in 1 John 4:5-6, the "Spirit of Truth" and the "Spirit of Error." The Spirit of Error is the source of all the "Strong Delusions" (2 Thess. 2:11) that are in the world today, and as the "End of the Age draws near they are being rapidly multiplied, and it requires the utmost vigilance not to be caught in their net. Just as the Church is indwelt and guided by the "Holy Spirit" so the world outside the Church is indwelt and guided by the "Spirit of the World" (1 Cor.2:12), or "Unholy Spirit." And as the "Holy Spirit" is a person so the "Spirit of the World" is a person. "And you hath quickened, (by His Holy Spirit), who were dead in trespasses and sins; wherein in time past ye walked according to the course Age) of this world, according to the Prince of the Power of the Air (Satan) the Spirit (Evil Spirit) that now worketh (energizes) in the— "Children of Disobedience." Eph. 2:1-2, from this we see that the "Spirit of the World" is Satan. The world refuse to accept the rule of God when it crucified His Son, and chose Barabbas instead of Christ, thus exalting Satan to the position of the God of this Age, for Satan is not spoken of as the God of any other Age than this. It was Satan's ambition to be like God that caused his fall (Isa. 14:13-14), and he has not yet given up that ambition, and it is his purpose and plan to exalt himself in the person of Antichrist, whom he will indwell, and sit in the "Temple of God," (the rebuilt Jewish Temple in Jerusalem), As God and have the people worship him as such. 2 Thess. 2:3-4, Rev. 13:4, 11-12. **MAN'S DAY,** This Dispensation is spoken of in the Scriptures as "Man's Day." Writing to the Corinthians Paul says, But with me it is a very small thing that I should be Judged of you, or of man's judgment. The margin reads o "Man's Day," 1 Cor. 4:3. This then is the day of Glorification of Man. The day in which the works of men are exalted and praised. We cannot explain the great advance in knowledge and the mechanic arts of the past one hundred years, apart from God, only on the supposition that there is some superhuman being who imparts this knowledge and who controls the affairs of the mechanical and commercial world.

The Kingdom of GOD vs The Kingdom of Devil

And it is worthy of note that it was not the descendants of Seth, the godly people of Antediluvian Dispensation, but the descendants of Cain, the ungodly people of that period, who invented mental working, devised musical instruments (doubtless for pleasure), and built great cities for commercial and other purposes. Now we know that Satan's gospel is the— "Gospel of Progress." He preached it in the Garden of Eden when he promised Eve that if she would eat of the fruit of the Tree of Knowledge of Good and Evil, her eyes would be opened and she and Adam would be as "God," knowing good and evil. Gen. 3:5. It was the promise of Knowledge that caused the downfall of the human race and when Adam and Eve followed Satan's advice they committed the race to the acceptance of his Leadership and Program. It is not likely that the Holy God imparted to ungodly race of Cain the knowledge to invent things that would lead to the downfall of the race and help to bring on the Flood. Neither is it to be supposed that a God of Love would impart to men the knowledge that would enable them to invent such a hellish instrument of warfare, as were used in the great European War. It is clear then that there is some "Supernatural Being" who is at the head of the "World System" and that "Being" is "Satan." His Program is to build up a magnificent Civilization without God. The phrase "Christian Civilization" is an invention of the God of this Age. There can be no such thing, for Christianity and Civilization have nothing in common. There can be no Christian civilization without Christ, and when He comes back He will bring to an end the boasted civilization of this Age, and set up a New Civilization over which Satan shall have no control, for he will then be a prisoner in the Pit. It is clear that if this world could be made a fit place for men to live in without God, it could not have had a more masterly leader than Satan, and that if he has failed it is not his fault, but is due to the willfulness of man. There are but two classes of people spoken of in the New Testament. The "Children of God" and the "Children of the Devil." In this the Children of God are manifest, and the Children of the Devil, whosoever doeth not righteousness is not of God. 1 John 3:10.

The Battle of the Culture

Here all who doeth not righteousness are classed as "Children of the Devil" and in Eph. 2:2 are called the "Children of Disobedience." There is no possibility of union between them, therefore there cannot be any such thing as the Brotherhood of Man, which popularly understood is the union of all religious bodies and sects, such as Christians, Jews, Atheists, Unitarians, Mohammedans, Buddhists Confucianists, etc., in a Federation of Religions. The word "disobedience" means obstinate rebellion. How futile then is the effort of the "Children of Disobedience" to make the earth a more comfortable habitation for man, and bring in a Millennium by a Federation of all Religious Bodies, when the bulk of mankind is in Obstinate Rebellion against God, and will not have His Son to reign over them, but are spending every energy to produce a "Godless Civilization" and make way for Satan's Masterpiece the Man of Sin. Satan is the Deceiver of the World. Rev. 12:9. He raises false hopes, and deludes by the—"Deceitfulness of Riches" (Matt. 13:22), the Deceitfulness of Sin (Heb.3:13), and the "Deceitfulness of Unrighteousness" 2 Thess.2:9-11. He causes the exercise of imagination and by strong delusion and seducing spirit; he tries to make men believe that his plans for the world's betterment are right. His advocates point to the great advance in methods of world-wide communication by land, sea, air and the various inventions that lighten labor and add to domestic comfort, and claim that the world is growing better, not only because of these, but because of the great philanthropies of men that have founded colleges, libraries, hospitals and great charitable institutions, forgetting that in spite of all this advancement of civilization, the world today sits on the mouth of a volcano, whose interior is a "foaming cauldron" of social unrest and commercial rottenness. When the "God of this Age" discovered that he could not stamp out the Church by Persecution, he changed his tactics and now seeks to neutralize her efforts by Seduction. His method is to divert her efforts for the evangelization of the world, to methods of "Social Betterment" and thus make the world a better place to live in forgetting that, as the natural man cannot be spiritually saved by **CULTURE**, neither can the world, therefore all efforts to save the world by "Social Betterment" are futile.

The Kingdom of GOD vs The Kingdom of Devil

And when the Church lends her aid to such methods she confesses that Christ's method of saving the world is INSUFFICENT, and thus discounts the power of the Gospel. Christian men and women give vast sums of money for Social Intellectual and Physical Betterment of the world, rather than for the evangelization of the world. They even go farther and form societies for the investigation of adverse social conditions, such as poverty, associations, ignorance, etc., and appoint specialists at high salaries to investigate and see if they can discover the cause of all the sin, misery and wretchedness there is in the world, forgetting that in so doing they are wasting their money, for the Bible told us centuries ago that the cause was Sin. If the proper thing to do is to remedy a thing at its source, let the Church apply the remedy of the Gospel and save the individual, and by thus doing save society. The common opinion is, that all the ills of society are in men's surroundings, or environment, whereas they are in man Himself Hence all human schemes for the Betterment of Society must begin in the **"MAN HIMSELF."** That is, man must first be regenerated by the Holy Spirit. All the schemes of men to make this world a better place to "Live In," seem to be to make the world a better place to "Sin In," because they increase the facilities for sin. The "God of this Age" knows that if the Church was to give herself exclusively to the work of "world Evangelization" he would lose her service in building his great "Civilization Structure," so he is just as anxious to keep her in his power, and postpone the time of her "Exodus," (1 Thess. 4:15-18), as Pharaoh was to keep Israel in Egypt at work on his stone cities Rameses and Pithom. To this end he keeps her busy "making bricks without straw," and thus blinds her eyes to the light of the "Glorious Gospel of Christ," (the doctrine of the Pre-Millennial Coming of the Lord), knowing that once she gets a vision of that she will refuse to any longer work for his "World Betterment" schemes. The unification of the nations of the earth is a scheme to reverse the judgment of God on Babel, and resume the building of "The Tower" that is to exalt the name of man. Gen.11:1-9. There are two "Distinct Bodies" in this "Present Evil Age" in the Process of formation. 1.) The "Body of Christ—the Church. 2.) The "Body of Antichrist."

The Battle of the Culture

The first is being gathered by the "Spirit of God" (Holy Spirit) 1 Cor. 12:3, 13, and the second by the "Spirit of Evil," that now worketh (energizes) in the "Children of Disobedience." Eph. 2:1-2. The difference between the "Body" the Holy Spirit is forming, and the Body the "Spirit of Evil" is forming, is that the former is united to a "Living Head," (Christ—Eph. 1:20-23), while the latter has no living head, for it is simply an "Organization," while the body of Christ is an Organism. Since the fall and death of Adam the human race has been headless, but when the Body or Organization, that the "Spirit of Evil" (Satan) is forming is complete, he (Satan) will produce its "Head," who will be the Antichrist, thus reversing the Divine order of first the "Head" (Christ and then the "Body"—the Church. We are told that the Lord at His "Second Coming" will depose and punish two distinct governing bodies. Isa. 24:21. 1.) "The High Ones that are on high." That is Satan and the "Evil Powers of Air." Eph. 6:12. 2.) "The Kings of the Earth upon the earth." That is the Anti-Christian World Powers represented by the "Ten Federated Kings" under the control of Antichrist. Rev.19:17-21. The heavens will then be cleansed of all the "Powers of Evil and their place will be taken and occupied by Christ and Saints who constitute the Church, and they will reign during the Millennium from the heavens over the earth, as Satan and hosts do now. Rev. 20:4.

CHAPTER III

IDENTITY CRISES

An identity crisis is a time in life when an individual begins to seriously quest for answers about the nature of his or her being and the search for an identity. Most persons go through periods of defiance against authority figures. Part of this "defining against" authority figures is identity crisis. Though kids may make extremely poor choices when they choose to defy parents, they are often participating in a deep exploration of self that will help them determine what they will do and who they will be as they enter adulthood. For parents, watching a child enter the identity crisis stage is often fearful and difficult, since deliberate disobedience to certain standards may be inherently risky. Kids can unfortunately wreck their futures if they push too far away from parental or societal law; they could end up addicted to drugs or parenting children of their own far before they're ready. Nevertheless, most children must make this fearful passage to find a unique identity. When they are in the midst of it, this may be called the moratorium stage. In this part choices are being evaluated and explored, and there might be high incidence of exploration or various ideas, interests, career, sexuality, and etc. Once through the crisis a person has what is called identity achievement. They have set their feet on a path and determined who they are and what they want to be. This isn't only about determining a potential career. Such a crisis can be about exploring sexual identity and deciding what ethics and values are most important. Some people end up on a path that determines their identity without exploration or introspection and this may be called a foreclosure state. Some social scientists feel that a foreclosure will precipitate an identity crisis at a later point, since little exploration about choice was made.

The Battle of the Culture

Occasionally people who live in very restrictive environments have their choice made for them, and an identity is established without much choice or examination of other options. There are certain cultures that deeply encourage and facilitate an identity crisis. In Amish cultures, some communities encourages older teens to live in the outside world before determining whether they will remain a permanent part of the Amish community and be baptized. Similarly, some Roman Catholic communities now have changed confirmation to a later time, or encourage people to take time to consider whether they truly wish to be confirmed in the Catholic Church. Allowing an identity to emerge before making such important decisions seems psychologically sound. As mentioned, the identity crisis is not redistricted to adolescence and the emergence into adulthood. It can occur at any time, and many people label the "Midlife Crisis" as a crisis of identity. Some people find their values, choice, or paths inappropriate after major life changes like a divorce. Furthermore, nations and communities can suffer these crises too communities can suffer these crises too as they grow or respond to major changes. How a culture identifies itself and what it wants and holds dear can be part of a national identity crisis that may take a while to resolve and may be somewhat constantly in flux. This brings us to God and who we are in Him. **Gen. 2: 15-18**… The Lord God took the man and put him in the Garden of Eden to work it and take care of it. And the Lord God commanded the man, "You are free to eat from any tree in the garden; but you must not eat from the tree of knowledge of good and evil, for when you eat of it you will surely die." The Lord God said, "It is not good for the man to be alone. I will make a helper suitable for him. **1 Cor. 9:3** Now, I want you to realize that the Head of every man is Christ, and the Head of every woman is man, and the Head of Christ is God. Before the fall of Adam and Eve God set the stage for them in the Garden of Eden in perfect form and atmosphere. In the Garden there was perfect peace in the family setting; Adam was given authority over the earth and in Adams authority notice in scripture God created Adam as a man and not a child or a boy because a child or a boy would not fit in such an atmosphere of authority.

IDENTITY CRISES

Only a man given authority by God would fit such a hierarchy position, **now there are five things God gave Adam 1.) Eden....2.), Work....3.) Cultivation....4.), Protection....5.) Gods Command...but there is five things God did first with male and that is 1.) the first human God created was the male, 2.) The first thing God gave the male was his image, 3.) The first place God place the male was in the Garden of Eden, 4.) The first assignment God gave the male was work, 5.) The first instruction God gave the male was cultivate.** Many of us coming up in looking at scripture believed that the first thing gave the male was dominion over the earth this is misinformation and has been the bases of the down fall of man's position and relationship on earth, is this attitude of authority first. If you study the scripture more carefully you would discover that the first thing God decided was not how much power and authority man was going to have, the first thing God decided was man's identity and What is man's identity? **"THE IMAGE OF GOD,"** It is in the image of God where all things in man starts, when a child is born the first thing parent identifies with is who the child looks like, as an teenager or an adult being a citizen of this nation of the United States it is a law that you obtain legal identification. Image is the essential key component of a man's life because image shapes character. As a citizen of the Kingdom of God being placed here on this earth you were given an identification to carry and be attached to you all the days of your life on earth and beyond **"THE IMAGE OF GOD."** This is to identify you as to what you are, why you are here, where you are going and How long you will be here. Adam was given the image of God, then instructions of what he was here for, Why he was here, Where he belong and how long he was to be in the garden "Eternally" (1000years), until an identity crises struck the garden. Devil embodied in the image of the snake sought to bring about a false identity, starting with Adams wife Eve. The Bible says that the serpent was more crafty than any beast of the field which God had made and he said to the woman— "Indeed, has God said, you shall not eat from any tree of the garden?"

The Battle of the Culture

The woman of the garden said to the serpent, "From the fruit of the trees of the garden we may eat; but from the fruit of the tree which is in the middle of the garden, God has said, You shall not eat from it or touch it, or you will die." The serpent said to the woman, "You surely will not die! For God knows that in the day you eat from it your eyes will be opened and you will be like God, knowing good and evil." This is called "Identity Theft" when one seeks to rob you of what you posses, that you no longer posses it. Devil sought to take away Adams identity by manipulating his wife Eve to switch from knowing only the image of God, which "Good" to now knowing his image "Evil." Gen.3:1-5. This is "The Battle of the Culture" where many of us do not know who we are as we carry out our lives here on earth. Too many false identities labeled upon us than the righteous identity "Image of God", we are to raped up into these mediocre labels such as "African American," "European American," Asian American," "Latino American" all these different labels we honor and display upon ourselves beyond the "Image of God." If you declare yourself to be of God, then you are a **"CITIZEN OF THE KINGDOM OF GOD,"** first before you are anything else. The reason Africa is called mother and not father is because you came through Africa not from Africa. When you are born of a woman you come through the woman's womb not from the woman's womb. Life comes from the seed of your father not the egg of the woman, so Africa is not a "SEED" it is an "EGG." This is why it's called mother and not father, because Africa incubates life not produces life, God produces life, not a piece of land. **I came through Africa, but from my Father in Heaven who is the "Author of Life."** So any label you give yourself outside the "Image of God" is a false label and should not have any authority upon your life unless it is from God who gave you the life you have. For His purpose not your own purpose and plan, you don't know enough about this life to have your own purpose and plan, this is why God says to the people of Israel— "For My thoughts are not your thoughts, Nor are your ways My ways," declares the Lord. "For as the heavens are higher than the earth, so are my ways higher than your ways and my thoughts than your thoughts. Isa. 55:8; 9.

IDENTITY CRISES

Once the fall of Adam and Eve too place, devil then presented a claim to Christ of owning the world as he said to Him— "I will give you all this domain and its glory; for it has been handed over to me, and I give it to whomever I wish. Therefore if you worship before me, it shall all be yours." Luke 4:6; 7. See, Devil committed identity theft upon Adam and Eve when the fall of them occurred because he was the cause of the "fall." This is the greatest level of theft that many people fast on a daily bases in this life is identity theft, having to deal with your name or your life being almost destroyed by such an act as this. The pain of the process to recover from such an act, pain in the initial thought process of the since of lost, which an overbearing mental pain that leads to a physical pain. This is how things play out in this "Battle of the Culture" when the Bible says— "We don't wrestle with flesh and blood but with spirits and principalities." Eph 6:12. The Devil seeks permission to attack our citizenship in the Kingdom of Heaven daily and his purpose is to keep us from knowing who we are in Christ. If we lose our identity in Christ, we lose ourselves; we lose ourselves on earth we lose our life from earth because at this point you are easily led to do anything as opposed to what the direction of God would be for the purpose he placed upon your life. It is very important to know your intimate purpose in Christ, your purpose and plan is all a part of the "Image of God," why so much the "Image of God" because you are the seed of your Father and being your Fathers seed is vitally important too whom you look like. If Devil can get you to believe in who you aren't as he did Eve in the Garden then it becomes temporarily powerful for him to get you not to believe in who you are the "Image of God" first before dominion. This is why many miss what God is seeking to do in your life because of misinformation, false information that one can't get beyond. So many people are misinformed on how God work; many are seeking to identify themselves with some sort of image in life that they themselves can identify with. It is in the image of things that one seeks his or her identity, in a mediocre world and because of image the world loses sight about who it was created by and for therefore the world falls into an Abyss by way of the hand of God.

The Battle of the Culture

Christ Jesus was sent for the restoration of the "Image of God" before freeing mankind from bondage, it was the image of God that appeared to be in more danger than man being in bondage. This is why the Bible says— "Meditate on God's word day and night, so that you may be careful to do according to all that is   written in it, what are we meditating on day and night, the overwhelming reason to such a high level of meditation is for purpose of God's Image. His Image as glorified as it is maintains all standards in your life know the level of intense character, integrity, discipline, obedience and righteousness such that this 'Image of God" carries it has no room for many crisis. Crisis come only by way of the opposite of what Gods image stands for and the opposite of God's Image is simple wickedness or foolishness. But often times God uses crisis to bring us to a point of obedience that "His Image" can shape our lives that looking upon us will see God in our thinking, our attitude, our speech, our behavior and our action. This is why crisis is important to identify, to know which way God is going with the use of the crisis in our lives, to know what the moment of the crisis is for, why the crisis exist and how to apply the wisdom of solution to the crisis that it "works for the good of those who love the Lord." A crisis is not something we have many answers too, we often fall short in dealing with crisis effectively enough that this crisis does not return the same way twice. Crisis must be met with head on with only God given wisdom, that the spirits and principalities that enforces a crisis can be met with very Holy Spirit that will give you the power of resistant's and the ability to overcome the obstacles that accompany it. You must not allow any room for crisis to over shadow the "Image of God" in you at no point for the sake of growth, progress, character etc. You must live your life in these last days as if Christ is returning tonight, seeking or pursuing God knowing He holds your life in the balance of His hands, under constant protection from the wolves, jackals and snakes. For any attack that comes to our lives must first get permission, can you imagine that, your enemy must get permission to put his hands upon you.

IDENTITY CRISES

What an awesome God we serve, **"I MEAN AWSOME."** You must know and understand meaning of a demonic spirit having to get permission to touch your life, do you understand how powerful that is, and the process a "Demonic Force" has to go through to get to you. What crisis could you possibly experience without the hand of God not being a part of things to protect your life. Identity Crisis is not a means of destruction; it's a means of opportunity, an opporture time in God obedience, discipline, character and integrity which should bring about a perfect union with God. But because of many not feeding the mind the proper level of God's word that your thinking is dealt with and changed so much so that discipline is the ruling aspect of your thought process. The main reason that we miss out on much of Gods directions in our lives is that we lack the kind of discipline in our thinking process, which would bring our decisions to a complete "YEA" and "NEA," anything beyond that is of the Devil the Bible says. Crisis should bring you growth from the level it began to the level it forces you to, why by force simply because of many of our stiff neck ways we allow to take root or stronghold in our thinking causing us to disobey Gods directions. The Bibles says— "Many are the plans in a man's heart but God directs his steps," Prov. 16:9. Crisis come by way of misinformation or no directions, we to many times find ourselves listening to our outer man instead of the inner man as the great "Marvin Gaye" would sing and that's where we fall in much trouble during the course of our lives. God continues to hammer away at our stubbornness to follow his instructions and many refuse to hear His voice or just not intimate enough with God to even hear His voice. Many bring about great damage control in their lives that in some cases it is beyond repair. We are in a time frame where it must be Gods way or you will be removed, we will begin to see that revolving door of the days when God remove you from for sin and those days are returning especially now that grace is on the scene through Christ. God no longer has to keep folk on earth to assure ones inheritage through a series of faith walks and prophetic deeds, Christ has covered all our sins of yesterday, today and tomorrow we no longer are in need of the New Moon Festival and Sin Offerings,

The Battle of the Culture

we have been sealed with the Holy Spirit that guarantee our salvation upon our confession of Rom. 10:9. So to remove those who are in great disobedience God will do and is doing to keep many from loosing portions of their inheritance. For it is your inheritance that is the only thing from Heaven that you will lose parts of and the Bibles says that God loves us so, that he protects us from taking great lost of our inheritance. The most powerful and richest place on earth is the cemetery simply because so many persons have left this earth without fulfilling the purpose God gave to many to serve here on earth. So many ideas, inventions, cure for diseases, answers to things in this life that would change the course of time forever. All in the cemetery not even an ounce of time to exercise such power and authority that was placed in these persons in the unique way they were created to exercise. So we lose those possibilities to bring about other persons with God given capabilities to exercise their uniqueness of gifting being shown to the world that the purpose of God can prevail. Prevail in a supernatural way that we can make great strive in this life just as God is calling us to have, not slothful or slumbered and full of poverty but making the difference in the lives of your family, friends and neighbors as we were chosen to do so. A nation of doers not a nation of Ney-Sayers but to conform in God that the world can spot who you are not by a cross on your neck or a bumper sticker, but in your speech, your walk, letting that spirit of God within us so connect to the Holy Spirit, that the directions and instruction given to us from God, by way of Christ in which direct the Holy Spirit to bring life into all things. We are to carry out the same as to what the Holy Spirit has been given because he is in us to do so, so that which is in you must flow out of you in righteousness that the world is affected by it so greatly that God is honored and Glorified in the Majestic manner that He demands. We are the Kings Royal Priesthood and we were chosen to operate in the "Image of God" and have dominion over this "Earth," **NOT TO CREATE AN IDENTITY CRISIS"**

IDENTITY CRISES

In this life we must not focus on our circumstances. That is a biblical principle that "you do not look to the bigness of your circumstances but look to the bigness of God, for if you look to the bigness of your circumstances then the Devil will use that moment against you and accuse you before God of lack of faith and belief in God to by o you to grace protect and bring you relief of that which stands in your way," We are to look past our circumstances in fact we are not too recognize our circumstances. We are to commit our lives so great too the purpose and plan that God has place upon you and live the meaning of that which God gave to carry out here on earth. Any and everyone has a purpose here and it isn't "Crisis," that is what is used to put us in obedience or discipline in God that character and integrity rules. You must live by meaning, What does your life mean to you? Is it a game or joke? Is it real? What is your name? Call your name and see what you are known by. These things are meaning, in my life I know I am to make a difference in the lives of others, that's something stuck with me all my life as I went through my daily routines of just getting up to go to a meaningless job. Faced with every day crisis I was lost in identity in my youth, but always had the spirit to help someone, something that I watch my "Mama" and my "Grandma" do. It was not something that I recognize as my purpose it was just something that was in me to do as the days of my life went forth as a youth. The day came when becoming a part of different communities and new persons arose in my life that I began to discover the meaning behind wanting to help folk. It began to unravel not in your typical world like fashion where you are in the streets and someone just think they know you well enough to tell you about your life "No." It came by way of the life I lived in God, see, I realize by way of the intimacy I have with God automatically gives the Holy Spirit the access it need to bring us wisdom even when we don't ask for it. You think you pick up on some high level of "ESP" as the world would say that gave you insight to the life we live, but the Bible says God through Christ Jesus is the author and giver of life period. Who else then can inform you of life but the author and giver of it?

The Battle of the Culture

As I began to investigate my life more it came to my attention that I have a real purpose here on earth and how did I find it, by the greatest question ever ask of me "What is your Passion in Life"? I stop a moment and had to put in some heavy meditation about that and of course the devil took root to that thought and began to squander my mind everywhere. I went after that question upon my own notion that I knew what I was searching for and found myself bringing on a headache, until I denied me and ask the Lord for the wisdom in this thing and as I began to remove me in thought. My though patterns began to open up to me and who I am and the thing I enjoy to do. That is help people, to make a difference in lives of people, I recognize the energy and strength I put into such a meaningful cause. Once I realize what this meant in my life, this was it, this is my passion, and this is my "Purpose." I began to feed this thing and bring it more to life as it must be, I studied Gods word on this and learn a deeper meaning on how it works from Gods point of view since He put it in me then the one to ask is the one who gave it "God," my life began to take a turn from "Identity Crisis" to "True Identity," the "Image of God." But once knowing this you would think life got better no, greater struggle, greater difficulty and greater attack. Why? Because we were in Devil's camp having a ball enjoying the world's lifestyle, chasing the wind of sex, lies and videotapes, festering in Devils mess, believing this was our way of life to live. When we were actually as to what the word of God says—whoever wishes to be a friend of the world makes himself an enemy of God. This is where we are when we are not with God, we are against God and that's the reason for attack, struggle and Identity Crisis, we lose sight of God and become someone we were not purpose to be and so the hand of God come against you is enemy. When you step out of Devils kingdom then you become an enemy of Devil, in other words there is no neutral zone between Gods Kingdom and Devils kingdom. You are in one or the other and either way you face difficulty, but the difference in Gods difficulty and Devils difficulty is with God difficulty come grace, peace and official rest as long as you remain in Him.

CHAPTER IV

RELIGION AND SCIENCE

What is Religion? Religion is a system of belief about deity, often involving rituals, a code of ethics, and a philosophy of life. Religion is an instigated institution of wars; Religion is man's search for God. God never gave Adam a religion when Adam fail he didn't lose a religion he lost a kingdom. When the kingdom was lost it was lost to Satan, Satan then began to manipulate the mind of man to introduce the two group religious theories, and the faith based theories and the secular based theories. According to some theologian historians **Faith based theories:** *A comparative survey of churches and religions - AD 30 to 2200,"* there are 19 major world religions which are subdivided into a total of 270 large religious groups, and many unique faith groups. Among this great religious diversity, there are probably hundreds of different religious creation stories which describe how humans, other species of life, the Earth, and the rest of the universe came to be.

The Battle of the Culture

Many of these stories describe the origins of their particular religion. It was typically based on revelation from one or more deities -- mainly gods and goddesses. **Secular-based theories:** Anthropologists, evolutionary biologists, and other researchers have reached a near consensus that humans of the species Homo sapiens evolved from a species of proto-humans who originated somewhere in Africa. (This statement probably upsets any white supremacists who are reading this essay. That can't be helped; scientists consider the evidence to be conclusive; ultimately, we are all descended from Africans.) These proto-humans walked upright, and had an opposing thumb and little finger. Their internal brain structure represented a major advance over those of previous animals in terms of its flexibility, its ability to reason, and its ability to plan for the future. This gave proto-humans an improved ability to pass on their accumulated knowledge to their descendents, to form more advanced societies, and ultimately to create religions. **Secular-based theories of religion:** Nobody knows with accuracy how the first religions evolved. By the time that writing had developed, many religions had been in place for many millennia and the details of their origins had been forgotten. However, there is speculation that the first religions were a response to human fear. They were created to give people a feeling of security in an insecure world, and a feeling of control over the environment where there was little control. **The developing abilities of proto-humans were a double-edge sword:** On the one hand, they aided their chances of surviving in a cruel and unpredictable world. They helped each successive generation of proto-humans to build upon the knowledge base of their ancestors. This increased mental ability led to a terrifying piece of knowledge: personal mortality. For the first time, individual animals on earth became aware that their life was transient; they would die at some point in their future. This knowledge produced an intolerable emotional drain.

Religion and Science

During their evolution from proto-human to full human, they developed questions about themselves and their environment:

- What controlled the seasonal cycles of nature -- the daily motion of the sun; the motion of the stars, the passing of the seasons, etc?
- What controlled their environment?
- What or who caused floods, rains, dry spells, storms, etc?
- What controls fertility -- of the tribe, its domesticated animals, and its crops?
- What system of morality is needed to best promote the stability of the tribe?
- And above all: what happens to a person after they die?

Living in a pre-scientific society, people had no way to resolve these questions. Even today, with all of our scientific advances, we still debate about the second last question, and still have no way of reaching a consensus on the last. But the need for answers (particularly to the last question) was so important that some response was required, even if they were merely based on hunches. Some people within the tribe started to invent answers based on their personal guesses. Thus developed: **The first religious belief system, the first priesthood, the first set of rituals to appease the Goddess**, Other rituals to control fertility and other aspects of the environment, a set of behavioral expectations for members of the tribe, and a set of moral truths to govern human behavior.

The Battle of the Culture

These formed an oral tradition which was disseminated among the members of the tribe and was taught to each new generation. Much later, when writing was developed, the beliefs were generally recorded in written form. A major loss of flexibility resulted. Oral traditions can evolve over time; written documents tend to be more permanent. Unfortunately, because these belief systems were based on hunches, the various religions which developed in different areas of the world were all different. Their teachings were in conflict with each other. Because the followers of most religions considered their beliefs to be derived directly from God, they cannot be easily changed. Thus, inter-religious compromise is difficult or impossible. Also, because religious texts are often ambiguous, divisions developed within religions. Different denominations, schools, or traditions have derived different meanings from the same religious texts. Thus were laid the foundations for millennia of inter-religious and intra-religious conflict, this in accord to what many historians speak of our various religions. One main aspect of the many religions is that in all it is simply a different path one has chosen to take to God. But yet true religion is as God says— "Those who consider themselves religious and yet do not keep a tight rein on their tongues deceive themselves, and their religion is worthless. Religion that God our Father accept as pure and faultless is this; to look after orphans and widows in their distress and to keep oneself from being polluted by the world, " this we as Citizens of the Kingdom of God to be true religion. This Gods religion and with Gods religion line this up to all so-called religions and see if they can stand up against Gods religion and watch the process of elimination. World religion was form to instigate destruction, because all that comes from these various religions is wars and rumors of wars out of different belief systems upon the four corners of the earth. Wars of the sword to conventional guns, and now high tech weaponry simply by way of one group of people, believing in something different than the other. This is a clear indication of the spiritual warfare that constantly goes on back and forth around us.

Religion and Science

This spiritual warfare constitute the many tribal rituals that we see in the continents of Africa and in many of your tribal areas of the world, these rituals give the falsehood to the belief systems that exist in many of these tribal rituals. Many of this ritual that was once accepted by God such as the sacrificial sin offerings, new moon festivals, the various foods too eat and not too eat etc. All until Jesus Christ was sacrificed on the cross that redeemed all mankind on earth from sin that then put away those rituals to now do all things through Christ who was given all power and authority in Heaven and on Earth to rule and govern the earth until the end of time that all power and authority be returned back to the Father God Almighty to be solely glorified as the all and one & only God. During the days of the great warrior Nimrod, the bible talks about the men of the east that Nimrod ruled the men of the east, with all speaking one language, thinking the same, attitude the same, behavior the same and actions the same. Until the day came that they began to build a tower, called "Babel" this tower was brought about for the purpose of Nimrods belief that it would allow the men of the east to escape the flood waters that God had cause on earth to destroy the earth do to the stench of sin that reached the nostrils of God. In his belief he thought such a tower would save them from such a flood occurring again but this is clear of the manipulation of devil over the mind of Nimrod, with him not knowing of the covenant that God declared with the symbol of the rainbow. This symbol indicating that God would no longer destroy the earth by water but by fire, if Nimrod would have accepted that from God he would not have to go through the trouble of building the "Towel of Babel," and so because he did this God spoke amongst the trinity in saying they must scramble these men in their language that they no longer understand one another in speech. And to send them all in different direction of the world, because there is nothing impossible the bible says they cannot do. So they went in many direction, devil on the other hand was seeking to set up a throne for himself using Nimrod and the men of the east in building this tower.

The Battle of the Culture

Simply that the tower is used as a throne in the heavens to duplicate God and His throne, but as the men of the east were scrambled devils plan was destroyed in which he gathered another plan now that the men are speaking different languages. This would be devils opportunity to bring about more belief systems and this time they would differ from each other that it would be design to weaken Gods purpose and plan on earth for the coming of time. This is not the start of religion over all the start of religion is when Satan was removed from the presents of God in Heaven. See, Devil being casted out of Heaven lead him to a great attack upon all man as to what was said when God ask him during the time of the attack on Job, when Satan entered in the realm of Heaven and God ask from where he came, he answered from roaming back and forth on the earth," Job. 1; As said in 1 Peter 5:8 "Be of sober spirit, be on the alert. Your adversary, the devil, prowls around like a roaring lion, seeking someone to devour." These are beginning moments of devil's assault to bring about an atmosphere of falsehood, lies and early destruction of the earth. This is the plight of religion, confusion and destruction of the human mind, that man does not accept the instructions given by God through His word. The concept of religion is a control factor of one lifestyle more over one's life, simply because devil knows that god seeks for us to develop a lifestyle on earth not life, we keep thinking we are to give our life to God on earth, when our lives already is God's. He gave us our lives to live here on earth so how is it that we are to give something to God that He already possesses. We need to understand the secret to all things on earth and the universe is the Trinity of the Father, the Son and the Holy Spirit reflected and expressed in the trinities of space, matter, time and man is the secret of the earth and universe. It is the key to many riddles of the universe. It shows why matter is what it is, of energy, motion and phenomena, with all their relationships. It shows why time is as it is, composed of future, present and past. It shows why man is a made as he. It may show the great unity the great principle of unity in all things. It should illumine the relationship of space, matter and time.

Religion and Science

It may well cast light on the mysterious principles of existence, of change and of reality, in the universe, may explain these universal things. It may make them clear, not as we ourselves paradoxically try to make mysteries clear, by involved effort, and intricacies of thought, and abstruse analysis, but by the broad, self-evident Fact of the Triune God. It is a world principle. It means for you, if you will, a new system of thought, a new way of thinking, based on the Image of God and of His Glory. It is, if you will, a true philosophy of things physical and things human. But better, it is a new vision of the universe, in the light of the Triune Image of God. No mind can think long and deeply upon the universe without asking a very great question. What is it which all things have in common? What makes this a universe? What is the basis of unity? Many feel that there must be a basis, science and philosophy both seek such a unity in all things, that basis is not the atom, nor the electron. Some have tried to find such a common basis of unity in the unit of matter, they have not only tried to explain the physical universe in that way, they have made even the human soul a combination or activity of atoms or electrons, or a series of reactions of mechanical forces. That effort is futile; the common basis will always seem and always be an artificial effort at unity. Neither can that common basis be seen as spirit, there are those who would see it so. They would view even the things of the physical universe as the apparently physical manifestations of pure spirit, many philosophies and many religions have attempt it, but it cannot be done. The common basis of the unity cannot be found in such unreal idealism, matter cannot be explained as spirit, and it is an artificial unity which such an effort brings. What is the basis of unity? The basis of unity cannot be a common stuff or a common substance, either physical or spiritual, it cannot be the materialist's unity or the idealist's unity, either atom or spirit. What is it? The answer to this question need be very self-evident one, and it must be something other than a common substance. There is for us a clear answer and a universal one, "Trinity," Trinity is what stars, trees, rocks, water, gases, light, heat, space, time, body, soul, daily life, consciousness and will all have in common.

Trinity, not vague and general, but of a very definite and exact kind, is what they all have and what they all are. It is a universal and unvarying basis of unity. This trinity in the likeness of God, this basis of unity, is seen to be not a common universal substance, but a common universal structure. The unity of all things, the unity of physical and spiritual things, cannot possibly, as we have seen, lie in a common substance. It is common structure; the search for a common universal substance is a hopeless one. It can succeed only by making the material world spiritual or the soul physical, trinity is far from fallacy, it is not a common substance, it is a common principle and structure of all things. Trinity in the image of the Three in One is that which all things have in common. It is the structure of all things, it is a basis of unity in all things, and may we say it is the basis of unity in all things, it makes this a universe.

UNIVERSAL SECRET OF SPACE AND MATTER

What is the relation between space, matter and time? That question must have hovered in our minds as we have thought about the three; it is indeed a question which is very much around us in the air today. The question of relationship or, as people like to call it, the relativity of space, matter and time, besets any thinking man or woman in recent years. What is the organic relationship of space, matter and time to each other? They are together the structure of the physical universe that of course we know they share a common vast trinity, each of them being a marvelous embodiment of it. That also we know but is there any other relation between them? Are these three trinities, which are the fabric of the physical universe, a yet vaster trinity explain and illumine the relationships of space, matter and time to each other? There are surely many mighty things which depend on it. Is space the source of matter? In the Divine Trinity the Father is the source of the Son, and the Son is the embodiment of the Father. In the trinity which calls matter, energy is the source of motion, and motion is the embodiment of energy. In the trinity of time, the future is the source of the present, and the present is perpetually becoming the embodiment of the future. In the trinity of man, the nature is the source and the person is the embodiment.

Religion and Science

Is it so then with space, matter and time together? Is space the source of matter? And is matter the embodiment of space? Are the relations between spaces and matter those of the universal trinity? We know what matter is, it is the energy, motion and phenomena, its chief factor is motion, but what is space? The answer is at once simple and complex, the simple answer is self-evident. We can all agree upon it, space is composed of dimensions that are certain, space is nothing else but it consists of dimensions. That is the clear and obvious answer but it is not answering enough for genuine reality such as we now would reach, we must go further. What then are the dimensions which we call space? What are they dimensions of? They are of course the dimensions of space, but that is tautological, it moves in a circle, they are the dimensions of space, but space, on the other hand is composed of these dimensions. A certain building is built of boards, you ask, "Boards of what? The answer comes "They are boards of the building." of course they are. But the building is composed of the boards, what are the boards composed of? Of Oak? Of Pine? Of Maple? So space is composed of dimensions, but what are the dimensions composed of? What are they dimensions of? Are they dimensions of nothingness, of absolute emptiness? That is a strange idea but stranger still, it is a very prevalent conception of space! Space is often described as nothingness and its dimension as dimensions of nothingness. But can nothingness have dimensions? You may indeed think of an empty box or chamber, and think of its emptiness as having dimensions. It might be emptied of air and contain only a vacuum, then there is nothing at all there, yet there are dimensions there. But in that case it is not the emptiness or vacuum which has the dimensions, it is the box or chamber which has the dimensions, and how can sheer, absolute nothingness have dimensions or anything else? The unreality of common idea of space as nothingness in several dimensions is strikingly shown by the revolt against it. That revolt, as we know regards space as being only a form of thought in which we conceive matter or motion, science of course is a sponsor for the idea that space is a form of thought in which the mind conceives matter.

The Battle of the Culture

But if in the day it had been clearly known through the advance of science that matter is essentially motion, and that this motion moves through incredible distances with inconceivable rapidity, that great thinker would probably not have held that space is purely a form of thought. For motion would exist if minds did not exist to think about it, and where motion is, there must be genuine extension and dimension, motion needs room, motion would create dimensions if there were none. Space is more than our way of conceiving motion. Unless all motion is a figment of the mind, the dimensions which we call space must be an outer reality. But what are Dimensions? What then are these dimensions? What is the reality of space? Are they the dimensions or motion? Is that ultimate reality, the basic fact of space? No, for motion is not basic, back of motion is energy, which passes into motion. Is energy basic then? Is that the primary thing, so that the dimensions of space were and are the dimensions of energy? No, for back of energy in the universe is whatever produces energy, wherever energy is there must be before it the power which produces that energy. There must be creative casual power out spread, before energy and motion were spread out in the universe, there was, and there had to be the outspread, omnipresent power which produces energy and motion. The dimensions which we call space were not primarily then the dimensions of energy, they go further back than that; they were the dimensions of that which produces energy and motion. They were the dimensions of outspread, universal, omnipresent Creative power in a universe with God in it. Is that ultimate? Did the dimensions which we call space exist before there was the presence of that Creative power? Was there ever a time when Divine power was not outspread and omnipresent, so that the dimensions of space were first of all the dimensions of nothingness? Are we thrown back after all upon that contradictory idea? There is no need of that impossible conception, for there never has been a time when there was nothingness and not God in the universe. There was never a time when His omnipresent power was not outspread everywhere, there is, therefore, no need to imagine that absurdity, a vast outstretching of nothingness in three dimensions.

Religion and Science

For there has always been the outspread power of God. The attempt to imagine a time before God existed, and to picture a vast emptiness in which His power was not present. But with an eternal God, and a God always present everywhere, the dimensions of the universe which now are visibly dimensions of motions, have always been primarily the dimensions of that Divine outspread power which precedes all energy and motion, those are the true and basic dimensions which compose space. ***"Real Space,"*** these dimensions are a reality, they are real space, space is not the absolute unreality which some would picture,—the outspreading of primal nothingness. Nor is space that practical unreality,—the outspreading of the mind to perceive matter or motion, for motion must precede its perception by the mind. And energy precedes motion. And Creative power outspread in dimensions precedes energy space then has always been the extension, not of the human mind, nor of motion, nor of nothingness, but of God's power. Space is reality, it is not nothingness in three dimensions, it is not a figment of the mind as it gazes upon motion, and it is reality. This is reality which we get from the principle of trinity as it points to space as the source of motion, how does power come to be a physical universe, but how does the outspread Creative power whose dimensions are space pass into a world of matter or motion? How do we get a physical universe? God is a Spirit, how does Divine power become physical? How does it pass into a tangible universe? That is one of the questions of thought, but the answer is clear, God's power is not only power to think but power to move. Can spirit move in a spatial way? Surely your mind is spirit and it can leap across the sea and pass to planets and stars. So, surely Creative power can move but as power to move that outspread Divine power becomes energy which is the power of physical motion. And this energy not only can move but as we know does move it becomes motion, everywhere, which manifests itself in all the phenomena of matter. It becomes a tangible universe, which we can feel and see and hear. ***The Reality of Space, Energy and Motion,*** then is not some vague way, but logically and truly, the basis and beginning of the actual, tangible universe.

The Battle of the Culture

It is not a framework, a location, vast nothingness in which in some way the universe is built; it is itself truly the basis and beginning of the physical universe. For this real and living space which is outspreading of Divine power into dimensions, is that by which such Divine power translates itself from spirit into energy and motion and so into a physical universe of energy and motion. But people may hesitate, this is not the way in which one has always thought about space, if one has been able to think about or conceive space at all either as physical nothingness or as mental unreality. This reality of space is however far more reasonable than the contrary and self-contradictory idea that space is nothingness, or a figment of the mind. It gives living reality to space and to the physical universe, and there is no reasonable objection to it. Can Divine power we ask, the power of God who is a Spirit, have dimensions? Surely omnipresence in a physical world must have dimensions, to some, too, this vision of space as the outspreading of Divine power may seem a more religious view than they are willing to sanction. But such a view of space is hardly unfitting in a theistic universe, a universe with God in it, and the only sane universe to sane mind. And it may be well to bring to mind how surprisingly this view of space fits in with the modern view of the physical universe as a universe of infinite activity, whose realities are not things or forms, but energy and motion. For nothing is inactive in the universe as we now know it—not even space! *How Modern Discovery Leads to This Reality* for this conception of space as the outspreading of Creative power, which passes, through energy and motion, into a physical universe, is remarkably confirmed by the general view of scientists today that matter is   essentially one of the form of light, of heat, of sound, of electric currents, of moving bodies of any radiation, of strains.   In all of these it is still energy, we can make it as solid as we will, and still it is one of the forms of energy. Solidity is an   impact made by energy upon our senses. In a very simple way we test this by experience, there before you is a body which we call a solid, you see it as a solid, that means that light rays, waves, energy, from it come with an impact upon retina of your eye.

Religion and Science

Now you touch and feel this solid object, that means that whatever the object is composed of makes impact upon your hand as your hand makes impact upon the object, and what you feel is the impact. Matter is the name which we give to tangible, audible, visible ways in which energy makes impact upon the mind through what we call the senses. Greater solidity is simply a greater proportion of particles of energy, of numbers electrons in each atom, making impact upon your senses; this is the whole tendency of "matter" as we go further into the analysis. The further we go, the more we find matter to consist essentially of energy, it consist as men of science agree of atoms. There are millions of atoms in the smallest visible particles of matter, they are moving at a tremendous rate of speed. The substance clearly grows less with analysis, the motion and energy increase. What are atoms? They consist largely of space, but within that space in each atom is a whirling galaxy of electrons, there are not many electrons in each atom, they are small that it is estimated that one of them is not more than one hundred trillionth of the size of the atom. But they move with inconceivable energy and speed, their speed is reckoned to be at least twelve thousand miles a second, they revolve we are told, around the nucleus at the centre of the atom a quadrillion times a second! Whether these figures will stand or not, the broad principle is clear, it means that the substance ceases, the energy becomes inconceivably great. We are not surprised that the physicist says that the electron is a particle of energy, and that it has no mass except its electric field, the electron can indeed be weighed, by its impact can be measured, for the impact of such energy even in such minute units, is very great enough, it is thought, to lift one hundred pounds one foot in one second. At least it is an impact of an incredibly minute particle of inconceivable energy, these electrons, it is believed revolve around a proton or group of protons at the heart of the atom, the proton is only one-thousandth of the size of the electrons which it holds in the orbits around it. But it is of yet more inconceivable energy perhaps two thousand times the energy of an electron, the particle grows immeasurably less!

The Battle of the Culture

The power grows yet incredibly more, the proton is a particle of positive electricity, the electron is a particle of negative electricity, negative and negative means simply that they are reciprocal or complementary manifestations of electricity or energy. An atom is simply a balanced number of particles or charges of electricity or energy, it is all energy, but now we come to yet infinitely smaller units, which all agree are pure energy. For the electron in its inconceivable whirl about the nucleus emits units of energy, it was said not many years ago that this was done by oscillation of the electron, now it is said that it happens when an electron shifts from one orbit to another or which is somewhat the same thing that it occurs when the electron drops from one energy level to another or that when an electron is stopped in its motion a unit or quantum of radiation is shaken off from it. And lastly it is said by a great physicist that all that we can be sure of is that these units of energy are emitted by some sort of atomic shiver or shudder and that we do not know just how it is done. In any case they are units of energy in strict and constant proportion to the frequency of the vibration in which they are propelled, because this proportion is a constant and because these are always units they are called quanta. They are the smallest units of energy which means the smallest units at all, which we now know in the physical universe, they are units of pure energy. No one thinks of them as anything but energy, the analysis of the matter then, by modern physics carries us far beyond substance into atomic regions where all is energy and power and we know that if the theory of protons and electrons, which are reasoned attempts to explain the energies issuing from the atom, should be discarded, we should still find ourselves before a world of atoms whose inner secret is one of vast and primal energy. Indeed there is a tendency to regard electrons as in no sense particles, not even of energy but simply as waves or impulses of energy. There are some who see atoms now as spheroid charges of electricity or energy, units of pure power. We know that if atoms, electrons and protons remain to us and are analyzed into the universe of yet immeasurably further from substance and yet immeasurably more in the presence of pure and apparently infinite energy and power.

Religion and Science

Or if the exact forms of atomic structure which science now pictures should be altered by further discovery, the whole tendency of discovery leads us to be sure in that case that we shall be yet more in the presence of immeasurable energy passing through inconceivable motion into the field of our senses. The whole tendency of modern physics leads us where we see on every hand omnipresent power and energy passing into a tangible universe of immeasurable motion. It is exactly as the principle of Trinity in the physical universe presents it to us. It is omnipresent, primal, outspread power passing through energy into physical motion which includes both the activities and the substance of the tangible world. ***How Ether leads to a New Reality,*** what someone may ask becomes of the scientific idea of "ether?" Does not this conception of space as the outspreading of omnipresent Divine power, which emerges through energy into a universe of physical motion, conflict somewhat with the conception of ether as a universal substance back of all other substances? It is true that the whole trend of scientific thought and discovery now conflicts with the conception of ether, to a far greater extent than many scientists realize. But the idea of ether makes certain very definite demands, which cannot be disregarded, yet the fact of space as the outspreading of Divine power, which emerges through energy into a universe of motion, though it conflicts with the conception of ether is confirmed in a remarkable way by the scientific demand for ether. For empty space in inconceivable ether, therefore a marvelous substance, alive with energy, is conceived, it must fill all space, it must provide in space between those concentrations of energy, between atoms, between protons and electrons, a medium for the transmission of vibrations or waves or quanta issuing from the atoms or for waves or impulses without atoms or electrons, if that should prove to be the reality of things. Clearly it must provide a medium for interaction between such concentrations of energy as protons and electrons may be and between atoms and surely between suns, planets and between stellar systems. By whatever name we call it, can energy carry across absolute emptiness?

The Battle of the Culture

A medium such as ether seems needed both for electric attraction across solar and stellar space, it seems needed to account for all these rays, vibrations, waves or quanta of radiated energy at the one universal speed which we know best as the speed of light. Even the upholders of the extreme New Science, the most earnest disciples of Relativity, although they discard absolute motion or motion with reference to the ether, regard ether as still a necessity. A leading and brilliant exponent of the new theories declares for instance— this does not mean that the ether is abolished, we need ether, and the physical world is not to be analyzed into isolated particles of matter or electricity to bear the characters of the particles. Characters such as mass and rigidity which we meet with in matter will naturally be absent in ether but the ether will have new and define characters of its own. The ether itself is a much to the force as it ever was in our present scheme of the world, but ether meets grave difficulties to transmit with such inconceivable momentum the vibrations coming to it must be a substance of enormous density. It must say the most careful scientific calculation, be at least a million times as dense as lead or platinum or any substance which we know. This is difficult enough to grasp or to believe, but to account as a concentrated substance for the weight of protons, ether, we are told by those who know must be of even more incredible density. It must be dense beyond all the power of science to imagine, but at the same time, to account for the vibrations per foot per second, ether must be a substance of almost infinite elasticity or resilience. That is equally demanded of it by scientific calculation, it must have that incredible density and then that immeasurable elasticity to overcome that density, each is beyond belief together in such incredible and almost infinitely contradictory combination, they stagger the intellect. These are the vast and contradictory demands which science makes upon ether as a substance, they mean insuperable difficulties, and two things however are clear; the factor in ether which provides for the activities of ether is its energy. The factor in ether which creates all these impossibilities of density and elasticity is its substance, why then imagine ether as a substance?

Religion and Science

Can we not get along with energy alone? NO, we cannot solve the problem as easily as that, if we could, ether as a substance would never have been conceived, there are great necessities to be met. In the first place, there must be continuity, a medium between the units or concentrations of energy, to transmit energy, whether as rays, vibrations, quanta or gravitation. There must also be a universal reservoir in which energy everywhere is latent and ready to leap into these activities and to concentrate into these units. There must also in any living activity, whether human or Divine, be a medium between spirit and matter, because of these necessities, ether is imagined as a substance to be a continuity, a reservoir, a medium even with all the impossibilities which such a substance creates. **The Way Out of Difficulty,** what then is the way out from the difficulty created by these demands, the answer is not impossible, do not the very demands reveal the way out from difficulty? Is not the true nature of the reality which we seek as ether found in the very nature of these demands? There must indeed be a medium between spirit and matter but there is a medium between spirit and matter. Power radiating from the Spirit of God or of man is always the medium between that spirit and all matter with which it deals. There must be a universal reservoir of energy, the energy which concentrates itself into protons or electrons or whatever units of energy we may find, but in a universe with God in it Creative power is the everywhere present reservoir of energy the source from which latent energy leaps into activity and concentrations everywhere in the universe. There must also be continuity, a medium, between units of energy, but such omnipresent Creative power itself, everywhere, outspread, the source of those units of energy is also the natural and logical medium between those units of energy which it produces, power, which produces protons, electrons, atoms and worlds and which where there are no protons or electrons, no atoms, no world, stands waiting, silent, invisible but everywhere ready to leap into instant energy and action and to transmit vibrations, rays, quanta, gravitation, is the perfect basis and medium.

The Battle of the Culture

Careful consideration will show that such power provides all that we can seek in the idea of ether; it provides much that we cannot seek in the idea of ether and it is free from all the objections to ether. For such universal power, passing into energy and motion provides beyond question for the discontinuity seen in protons and electrons, they are normally and inevitably seen as concentrations of power and of the energy into which it passes. They are essentially particles of energy, no other qualities have been found in them, for the weight of protons is simply the impact of their enormous energy. The mass of protons or electron is simply the mass of its electric field, even if we give these particles substance, the substance is simply a form which their concentrated energy assumes, they are concentrations of power which produces that energy. And no impossible density is needed in concentrated power as the stuff of which protons and electrons are made. It is reasonable to ask, does the being of the Creator, which explains so much about His creations, and especially about that wonderful creation, man, explain the creative work of man himself? Certain factors are always found in all creative work of man. Always there is and has been debate about them, why are they as they are? What is the principle of them all? What is the unity of them all? And there is the further question, which of these factors is most vital? It is an endless question, pro and con. The factors themselves are known to everybody, they are found in some degree in every creative work. 1). the source—the idea—the picture—the conception— the ideal—the inspiration. 2). The embodiment— the picture— the poem— the sonata— the song — the statue— the building. 3). the picture, poem, song as it affects and moves others. It is always these three factors, whatever the creative work— whether Hamlet or a children's tale, whether the Last Supper or a sporting print, whether or a folk song or a popular statue, whether the Taj Mahal—always these three! Why are they as they as they are, — always these three, — the source or idea, the thing which embodies the idea the thing working in the souls of others? Because the universe is so because matter, time, man and the process of existence and the principle of progress and the principle of reality are so.

Religion and Science

Because the Creator and ground of the universe of space, matter, time and man— the Creator of the creative energies of man— is God the Father, the Almighty Source and God the Son, the marvelous Embodiment and God the Holy Spirit, who moves in the souls of men. Which of these three factors in man's creative work is the most vital? That is the basis of vast discussion, whole of art has arisen from this or that emphasis upon one factor or the other. Whole schools of theory have hung on this factor or that, which is the most vital factor? Some say the idea and truly we must have the idea, without it there is but an exhibition of technique. We all know the things without an idea, the galleries of dead but unburied paintings, the machine-made popular songs the verse which generation ago was sounding brass and tinkling cymbals. The endless streets of dull or smart complacency, we must have the idea the inspiration. But we must have power to embody the idea, else it is not art, it is impulsive amateurism, many any fail in that way. We must have technique to embody the inspiration in well-painted picture, in well-wrought poem, in well modeled statue, in well-proportioned building. But the picture, the poem, the song, the statue, the building must touch and influence others. What matter how beautiful it is, if it has no spell for the souls which see or hear it! What use its power, its idea, its technique, if it leaves all other minds cold! We must have the idea,— we must have the technique, — we must have the instinct for other minds. The picture, the poem, the song, must live in other lives. Which of these is most necessary? Which is most vital? The answer lies deep in the nature of things, in the being of God— the ground of the universe— Father, Son and Holy Spirit are so deeply One that no one of the three can exist without the other two and no two can exist without the third. The three dimensions of space are so much one that no one of the three can exist without the other two and no two can exist without the third. Energy, motion and phenomena in matter are so much one that no one of the three can exist without the other two and no two can exist without the third. Past, present and future in time are so much one that no one of these three can exist without the other two and no one of the three can exist without the other two and no two without the third.

The Battle of the Culture

So also nature, person and personality in human existence are so deeply, one that no one of these three can exist without the other two and no two without the third. And so also it is of human creative work, that no one of the three factors in it can exist without the other two and no two without the third, it is the unity of life, with any of the three lacking, there is no life and no art. The uninspired creation is dead from its birth, the inspiration poorly wrought out is an ambitious failure. The work of art which makes no contact with other minds might better have been born, but when the three cooperate, there is life and victory. The inspired idea, the source—working through the perfect embodiment, the visible audible reality enters into its mighty influence, its living presence, in the souls of others and this principle rises also into the realm of the universal reality. It leads to the problem of Aesthetics, a universal problem, above and beyond all individual works of human creative art. Where is beauty? In what does it reside? That is the Aesthetics, some say that beauty lies in the ideal, the abstract, which the visible or audible object embodies, that is the view of the Platonist, he sees the ideal as existing in all its perfection, bright, ineffable, never wholly to be toughed above and before its appearance in any individual embodiment of it. This is what the Idealist holds, some say that beauty lies wholly or mainly in the object, the work of art or of nature, the statue, the symphony, the tree, the sunset, which we see or hear. That is what the Realist says, beauty seems to him wholly objective, and the ideal is to him something which we construct from the definite things of beauty which we see or hear. He is not sure whether the ideal truly exists, certainly the specific thing of beauty is the most real to him; some say that beauty is in the mind of the beholder or hearer, certain things give him pleasure. Certain things give him delight, these he calls beautiful, beauty then, he is ready to say and to demand that we should admit is in the mind the beholder, it is a pure subjective quality. That is what the Romaticist may say; it is what the Pragmatist does say, which is right? Where does beauty reside? In the ideal? Or in the embodiment, the object? Or in the mind of the beholder? Which is right? And what is reason for it?

Religion and Science

All are right. Beauty resides in the abstract, we can easily test it, and we cannot follow the processes of the Divine Creator of the sunset, the mountain height or the flower. But we can follow our own processes, the artist or the artificer who would create an object of beauty, a picture, a song, a sonnet, a vase, without an ideal glowing before him, a vision of what he would like to embody in his work of art, will fail to capture beauty and fix it there. Beauty dwells in the ideal and beauty dwells in the object which we see or hear if it is not there, the beholder or hearer will surely never know the ideal which is dimmed and concealed by the unbeautiful work of art. The artist must have his vision, it is true, but he cannot show it to us except in the beauty of work which embodies it, beauty dwells in the visible object the work of art or of nature and beauty lives in the mind of the beholder or hearer and would have neither meaning nor reality without its place in the mind of the beholder or hearer. There must be the thrill, the must be the delight, there must be pleasure, there must be the emotion, if there is nothing of these in any mind as it sees or hears the work of art, where for us is the beauty? How has it any reality? Beauty dwells in the soul of the beholder or hearer. Beauty dwells in all three— in the ideal, in the individual embodiments, in the mind of the beholder and no one of three can be the home of beauty or sub-limit without the other two. Why does beauty dwell so in all three: the ideal, the embodiment, the mind of the beholder? Because this universe of beauty takes its character from the Creator and ground of the universe and reflects the beauty and sub-limits of His being, He is the Image, the Father, the source, revealed by the visible or audible embodiment. And He is the visible one, the Son, embodying the Father, and He is the Holy Spirit, who moves in the hearts and minds of others and all three are one in an infinite, intensive, almighty Unity. **Goodness, Truth and Beauty,** these three ideals or facts means much to many thinkers today, here we see them in the forms of Ethics, Reality and Aesthetics, each of the three goodness, truth and beauty is a perfect reflection of the Divine Trinity of the Father, Son, and Holy Spirit.

The Formula of the Universe, the universe of the matter, time of man, of man's creative work, of sub-limits, beauty, space, matter, time, of the process of existence, of change, changelessness, of reality, is one universe truly a universe with one pattern, one organic law, built in the likeness of its Creator, The Father, The Son and The Holy Spirit—three in one. And if to say that the universe reflects its Creator seems to any highly sophisticated mind too simple or too romantic and something more abstract seems desirable, put it in this way— that this which we clearly been discovering in one realm after another is clearly the formula of the universe and that this formula naturally and inevitably coincides with the principle of the Image of God, who is the Ground of the Universe.

Which Explains Which?

The Divine Trinity (Trinity) explains these universal things, but these things do not explain that trinity, the structure of the universe, the nature of space, of matter, of time, of human life, attest the Trinity. They reflect the Trinity, they demand but while they do all these things, they do not explain trinity, the trinity explains them. Someone will try to turn this whole revelation around and argue that the father, Son and Holy Spirit are the effort of some long-ago thinker to out this universal trinity into theistic form. It will be so argued by someone who does not personally know the Trinity of God. The answer to such an effort is as we have said before, overwhelming, 1.) There is no sign of such an origin in the Biblical presentation of the Trinity. 2.) No man or men could build out of this universal trinity such matter-of-fact and natural and almost casual and wholly untheoretical presentation of Father, Son and Holy Spirit 3.) There is no reason to think that any man in New Testament days knew or could know this scientific, universal trinity. 4.) Above all, such an explanation does not explain this universal trinity itself, in space, in matter, in time, in all three together, in human existence, in human self-realization, in human self-direction, in the laws of reality, in the process of the universe. This universal trinity has a cause, if this is an orderly universe, if this is a theistic universe that cause must be in God.

Religion and Science

Such trinity in God is not the result of the universal trinity, it is the cause, for that is what the universal trinity and that is what the New Testament Trinity demands as its explanation. It can have come only from the trinity which the whole universe reveals in God, the universal trinities therefore in space, matter, time and in other universal things, do not cause and do not explain the Divine Trinity. But the Divine Trinity alone could cause and alone explains these universal trinities; the reason of the universe is the universe as it is because of some special plan which requires that the universe should be so? Or is the universe as it is from some inherent necessity? These great questions disappear in the light of an answer deeper and greater than either, it is not simply a special arbitrary plan, chosen out of endless possibilities. Nor is it on the other hand simply necessity in the nature of the universe itself, it lies far deeper; the universe is as it is because it naturally and inevitably reflects the being of its Maker and Worker. That means indeed a plan of the universe, but not an arbitrary plan; it means a necessity, but a necessity far deeper than anything in the nature of the universe itself. The universe inevitably reflects the being of its maker and Worker, He creates it upon lines of His own being, and He perpetually creates it and works in it in harmony with His own being. He expresses, it is the visible vesture conformed to His own mighty being the Divine Method of work, all these trinities are the workings of an imminent God. He is not merely the Creator, He works now in His universe, these things are His method of working, they are not static, they are not fixed and hard, they are His living method of working. The relation between energy, motion and phenomena or between future, present and past or between space, matter and time, or between nature, person and personality is an active relation. It is not merely an architectural relation between the three in each of these trinities. It is an active relation, these things are not buildings, they are processes, it is a working relation, and it is the immanent God working through motion and phenomena. He works from future through present and past, He works from space through motion or matter and time, He works from nature through person and personality, and they are His constant and active method.

He works through these trinities in His universe; they are not merely a passive reflection of Him in a fixed and universal mirror. Your mirror reflects you but far better and more truly your ways of work reflects you, these trinities reflect God not only as the passive mirror of creation reflecting the Creator. They reflect Him as your ways of work reflect you; they are the triune methods of the Triune God working in His universe, as Creator He is reflected in them, as the Worker in His universe He shines through them. **The Deeper Mysteries and the Universe**, so all explaining is the light of the Divine Trinity of God in His universe that even the deeper mysteries of that Trinity cast a revealing light upon the mysteries of the universe. What holds the universe together, so that it works as one immeasurable whole? What holds the stars in their order and harmony? What keeps them in their orbits? What holds the atoms in order? What holds electrons in their orbits around the proton in the in electrons in their orbits around the proton in the infinitesimal solar system which we call the atom? The only answer which has never been given at all is the answer of the Bible, that in Him— the Son (the second person of the trinity), the Creator— "all things hold together or consist." What holds the mind together in the yet more wonderful inner universe? What holds intelligence, feeling, willing, memory, and imagination together in order and harmony in the mind? The only answer which has ever been given or ever attempted is the answer of the New Testament, that in Him the Son, "all things hold together." It means that the Creator, the Son, holds atoms, stars, forces of nature, forces of the mind, things visible and things invisible," the whole vast universe together in order and harmony in life and unity. If this mighty answer is true — and certain it is that no other answer has ever been given, then the universe centers in the Son, the same New Testament which brings to us that Divine Trinity of the Father, Son and Holy Spirit which the universe requires depicts also the universe as centering in the Second Person of that trinity. But if the universe centers in the Second person of the Trinity, should not the reflection of the Divine Triunity in the universe be primarily a reflection of the Son? Would not that be strange?

Religion and Science

Yes, but so it is, the Image in each of those great trinities which make up the universe is above all an image of the Son! The emphasis is upon Him in all of these universal reflections of triunity. Nature and Personality centre in the Person, they are both invisible, it is the Person which we see and know, Future, Past centre in the Present; it is the Present which alone we can tough and know. Energy and Phenomena centre in Motion, Space, Matter or Motion and Time centre in Matter or Motion, Space and Time we know only through Motion or Matter, the second factor is not greater than the other two, but it is the most vivid and so the first and third elements centre in it. It is motion, in energy, motion and phenomena— it is the presents, in future, present and past,— it is matter or motion, in space, motion and time,— it is person, in nature, person and personality — which is central and most vivid. And now we see the reason, it is not because the Son is greater than the Father or the Spirit; it is because the universe in its vast triunity reflects most vividly the Second Person in the Three in One, the Son, and the Creator, in whom all things consist. A yet deeper mystery the Bible declares in regard to the Divine Triunity and yet it fits the facts of the universe and cast light upon these mysteries of the universe which we know only too well. The Bible declares, in the Book of Revelation that "at the end" "the Son shall deliver up the Kingdom of God, even the Father." This is to be when He, the Son, shall have abolished all rule and all authority and power, it alludes to the power of every evil authority or force and to the power of death. For He, the Son, must reign til He hath put all His enemies under His feet. The last enemy that shall be abolished is death, this evidently means all that force of death and destruction, both in human life and in the universe at large, which negatives God's whole creative purpose and work. "And when all things have been subjected to Him, that God may be all in all," a profound mystery, but a profound illumination! We see it going on now, sin; disorder and destruction permeate the universe now. The Son, the Creator, Himself enters the life of the universe in a peculiar and personal way, He does it entering as a Person, the life of the human race, He becomes man, He overcomes sin, He does this in His own life for thirty-three years.

The Battle of the Culture

He does it for mankind, the Bible declares, by His Personal death and resurrection, and then He works in men, the key to the whole vast situation, by His Spirit. At last "at the end," He brings all things into subjection, a new created race emerges from every tribe and tongue and people and nation. A new universe, no longer groaning and travailing in pain, New heavens and a new earth, "all things new," sin and evil and destruction cast out from it all, then at all things are in harmony with God, the nature of God at last holds absolute sway in the universe. The redeeming, reorganizing, recreating work of the Son is done, no longer must one of the Three in One make it His work to reclaim the universe from sin and disaster, God, the three in One, the one in three, is at last all in all in His universe. But now, as we can see everywhere in the universe, as we have been seeing in one realm of the universe after another, it is the Son in the Divine Trinity who is above all reflected, it is He who is reflected in the vast interwoven fabric of Motion. It is He who is mirrored in the living Present, it is He who imaged in persons, and it is through Jesus, the Son, that we came to know that whole Divine Trinity to us. To know Jesus is to know the Secret of the triune universe, He is the key to the great mysteries and realities of God and the great mysteries of the universe of space, of matter, of time, of the relations of space, matter and time, of human existence, of the process of all existence, of the law of all progress, of the forms of reason, of "being" and "becoming," of the unity of all things and of countless mysteries yet to be revealed. He is the key in who are all the treasures of wisdom and knowledge hidden, **The Riddle of the Universe and its Almighty Answer**, the riddle of the universe brings its own universal answer, and the riddle leads to reality. Why are all things what they are? Becomes Why are space and matter and time and space, matter and time, human existence, progress, moral action, reality, beauty, all triune, in exactly the same sort of way? And by its universal corroboration and its universal demand the riddle leads directly to its own answer in the triune God. That is as it should be what else but the being of God could explain His universe?

Religion and Science

He is the cause of all its triune structure; He is the worker in all its triune methods. He is the solution of all its triune mysteries, who knows what wonders we may yet discover, beyond all the wonders of modern science, in the natural world and the inner world, when we have learned to see and interpret the universe in light of its Triune God? How many decisive formula to unlock new resources of power, lie undiscovered in the triune Formula of the universe? How many far-reaching principles may radiate from the triune Principle of the universe? How many processes of value to men, may reasonably be produced from the Process of the universe? And surely the more we penetrate into the secrets of personal being, in our intense modern study of human life, the more we penetrate into the secrets of personal being, in our intense modern study of human life, the more we must see as their secret the Triune being who upholds the universe and in whose likeness and reflection man is what he is. We may escape the danger, which now threatens us, that our immeasurably growing knowledge of the physical universe may overwhelm us— if only we will learn to see the natural world in the light of its Triune God. We may escape, too, the greater danger of the present day, in our over-eager study of our own being, our actions and reactions, our behavior, our thinking, our reason and everything else about us, that we shall analyze ourselves into conceit, inbreeding and ineffectiveness and the deification of man— if only we will see human existence always in the light of its Triune God. Is it too much to say that all things lie open to the thinker who knows the Triune God and who dares to apply the supreme fact of the universe to the other facts of the universe? And what greater things are open to him who applies it to his own life? There lies indeed the way of vision and power, for life is greater than thought and know truly the triune God is life indeed. So why then do "Science or the World Questions God"?

CHAPTER V

QUESTIONING GOD

GODS WORD! The Bible is not a systematic treatise on Theology, or Morals, or History, or Science, or any other topic. It is the Revelation of God, of the Fall of Man, the Way of Salvation and of God's "Plan and Purpose in the Ages." It treats of **1.) Four Persons— God the Father, God the Son, God the Holy Spirit and Satan 2.) Three Places— Heaven, Earth and Hell. 3.) Three Classes of People— the Jew, the Gentile (also known as the nations), and the Church of God.** The Scriptures were given to us piece-meal, "at sundry times and in divers manners," Holy men of God spoke as they were moved by the Holy Spirit, during a period of 1600 years, extending from B.C. 1492 to A.D. 100, the Bible consists of 66 separate books; 39 in the Old Testament and 27 in the New Testament. These books were written by over 40 different authors, by kings such as David and Solomon; by statesmen, as Daniel and Nehemiah; by priests, as Ezra; by men learned in the wisdom of Egypt, as Moses; by men in Jewish law, as Paul. By a herdsman, Amos; a tax-gatherer, Mathew; fishermen, as Peter, James and John, who were "unlearned and ignorant" men; a physician, Luke; and such mighty "seers" as Isaiah, Ezekiel and Zechariah. It is not an Asiatic book, though it is written in that part of the world, its pages were penned in the Wilderness of Sinai, the cliffs of Arabia, the hills and towns of Palestine, the courts of the Temple,

The Battle of the Culture

the schools of the prophets at Bethel and Jericho, in the palace of Shushan in Persia, on the banks of the river Chebar in Babylonia, in the dungeons of Rome, and on the lonely Island of Patmos, in the Aegean Sea. Imagine another book, compiled in a similar manner, suppose, for illustration that we take 66 medical books written by 40 different physicians and surgeons during a period of 1600 years of various schools of medicine, as Allophathy, Homeopathy, Hydropathy, Osteopathy, etc., and bind them all together and then undertake to doctor a man according to book, what success would we expect to have and what accord would there be in such a medical work. While the Bible has been complied in manner described, it is not a "heterogeneous jumble" of ancient history, myths, legends, religious speculations and superstitions. There is a progress of revelation and doctrine in it, the Judges knew more than the Patriarchs, the Prophets than the Judges, the Apostles than the Prophets. The Old and New Testaments are not separate and distinct books, the New taking the place of the Old and the Old is "unfolded" in the New, you cannot understand Leviticus without Hebrews or Daniel without Revelation or the Passover or Isaiah 53 without the gospels of Matthew, Mark, Luke and John. While the Bible is a revelation from God, it is not written in a superhuman or celestial language, if it were, we could not understand it. Its supernatural origin however is seen in the fact that it can be translated into any language and not lose its virility or spiritual life giving power and when translated into any language it fixes that language in its purest form. The language however of the Bible is of three kinds, Figurative, Symbolical and literal such expressions as "Harden not your heart," "Let the dead bury their dead," are figurative and their meaning is made clear by context. Symbolic language, like the description of Nebuchadnezzer's "Colossus," Daniel's "Four Wild Beast," or Christ in the midst of the "Seven Candlesticks," is explained, either in the same chapter or somewhere else in the Bible. The rest of the language of the Bible is to be interpreted according to the customary rules of grammar and rhetoric, that is, we are to read the Bible as we would read any other book, letting it say what it wants to say and not allegorize or spiritualize its meaning. It is this false method of interpreting Scripture that has led to the origin of so many religious sects and denominations, there are three things that we must avoid in handling of God's Word: **1.) The Misinterpretation of Scripture.   2.) The Misapplication of Scripture. 3.) The Dislocation of Scripture.** The trouble is men and women are not willing to let the Scriptures say what they want to say, this is largely due to their training, environment, prejudice or desire to make the scriptures teach some favorite doctrine. Then again we must not overlook the "Parabolic Method" of imparting truth, Jesus did not invent it though He largely used it, and it was employed by the Old Testament prophets. In the New Testament it is used as a "Mystery Form" of imparting truth. Matt, 13:10-17, A mystery is not something that cannot be known, but something that for the time being is hidden, I hand you a sealed letter, what it contains is a mystery to you. Break the seal and read the letter and it ceases to be a mystery, but you may not be able to read the letter, because it is written in a language with which you are not familiar, learn the language and the mystery ceases. But perhaps the letter contains technical terms which you do not understand, learn their meaning and all will be plain, that is the way with the Mysteries of Scriptures, learn to read them by the help of their author, the Holy Spirit and they will no longer be mysteries. This brings us to the great question— **Is The Bible God's Book or Man's Book?** That is, did God write it, or is it simply a collection of the writings of men? If it is simply a collection of the writings of men, without any divine guidance, then it is no more reliable than are the writings of men; but if God wrote it, then it must be true and we can depend upon its statements. It is clear from the character of the Bible that it is not the work of man, for man could not have written it if he would and would not have written it if he could. It details with scathing and unsparing severity the sins of its greatest men, as Abraham, Jacob, Moses, David and Solomon, charging them with falsehood, treachery, pride, adultery, cowardice, murder and gross licentiousness and presents the history of the Children of Israel as a humiliating record of ingratitude, idolatry, unbelief and rebellion and it is safe to say that the Jews unguided and undirected by the Holy Spirit, would never have chronicled the sinful history of their nation. How then was the Bible written? The Bible itself gives the answer. **"All Scripture Is Given by Inspiration of God." 2 Tim. 3:16. I. What are we to understand by the "Inspiration" of the Scripture?** We are to understand that God directed men, chosen by Him to put into writing such messages, laws, doctrines, historical facts and revelations, as He wished men to know. All scripture (the Graphed writing), is given by inspiration (The op-neu-stos), that is, is— **GOD BREATHED.** That is, God Himself or through the Holy Spirit told holy men of old just what to write, the Bible, then, is the Word of God and does not simply here and there contain it. God is a Person and can both write and speak, He wrote the two "Tables of Testimony" on stone, Ex. 31:18; 32:16 and on the wall of Belshazzar's Palace. Dan. 5:5, 24-28, He talked with Moses on the Mount when He gave him the Specifications for the Tabernacle and its furnishings and all the Levitical Law and order of service. He spoke at the Baptism of Jesus (Matt. 3:17) and on the Mount of Transfiguration, Matt 17:5 and one day when Jesus was talking to the multitude, John 12:27-30. But God not only spoke directly to men, He spoke to them in the person of Jesus, for Jesus was God Manifest In The Flesh. John 1:1-5, 14. I Tim. 3:16, Matthew and John's Gospels contain 49 chapters 1950 verses, 1140 of which, almost three-fifths, were spoken by Jesus and He claimed that what He spoke, He spoke not of Himself but that the Father which sent Him, gave Him commandment What He Should Speak. John12:49, 50. We see then that God can both write and speak and therefore can tell others what to write and speak. **II. Does the inspiration of the Bible Extend to Every Part?**

QUESTIONING GOD

Yes, from the dry lists in Chronicles to the very words of God in Exodus and through Christ and more, it extends to every sentence, word, mark, point, jot and tittle in the original parchments When Jesus said in Matt. 5:17,18 That not one "Jot" or "tittle" should pass from the Law until all be fulfilled, he referred to the smallest letter (jot) and the smallest mark (tittle) of the Hebrew language, thus indicating that even they were inspired and were necessary for a complete understanding of God's meaning in His Word. But how about the words of Satan and wicked and uninspired men, the genealogical tables and the account of the Fall of Man, the Flood and other historical portions of the Bible. They were inspired of record. That is, the inspired penman or historian was told what historical facts to record and what to omit, to one who has read the Old Testament and also profane history covering the same period with its legends and traditions and detailed descriptions, it is very clear that the writers of Old Testament were divinely inspired to record only those things that would throw light on God's and Purpose in the Ages.

III. How were These Men Inspired to Write the Scripture? Were they simply thrown into a kind of "spell," or "ecstasy," or "trance," and wrote under its influence whatever came into their mind or did God through the Holy Spirit, dictate to them the exact words to use? We know that thought can only be expressed in words and those words must express the exact thought of the speaker or writer, otherwise his exact thought is not expressed. We see then that inerrancy demands that the sacred writer be simply an amanuensis. This we see is what the Scriptures claim for them, In II. Pet. 1:20, 21 we read that— "No prophecy of the scripture is of any private interpretation," that is, no man has a right to say what the Scriptures, according to his opinion, means. Why? Because— " The Prophecy came not in old time by the will of man, but holy men of God spake as they as they were Moved by the Holy Ghost," and this confirmed by the fact that much that the Old Testament Prophets wrote they did not themselves understand, I. Pet. 1:10,11. They must then have been mere amanuenses, recording words that that needed an interpreter, that they were mere instruments is shown by the fact that not all of them were good or holy men,

The Battle of the Culture

as Balaam (Num. 22:38; 23:26), King Saul (I Sam. 10:10-12; 19:20-24), the Prophet of Bethel (I Kings 13:7-10; 20:22;26), and Caiaphas, John 11:49-52. That the Old Testament writers spake and wrote the exact words that God gave to them is clear from their own statements, Moses declares that the Lord said unto him— " Now therefore go and I will be with thy mouth and teach thee what thou shalt say," Ex. 4:10-12 The Prophet Jeremiah says— Then the Lord put forth His hand and touched my mouth, and the Lord said unto me, Behold, I have put my Words In Thy Mouth." Jer. 1:6-9. Ezekiel, Daniel and all the prophets make the same claim, the expressions — "The Lord said," "The Lord Spoke saying," "Thus saith the Lord," etc., etc., occur 560 times in the Pentateuch, 300 times in the Historical and Prophetical books, 1200 times in the Prophets (24 times in Malachi alone), in all over 2000 times in the Old Testament, thus proving the statement of Peter, that Holy men of God Spoke as they were moved by the Holy Ghost. But you say— "If this be true how do you account for the difference of style of the writers; for Isaiah's style is different from Ezekiel's or Daniel's and Peter's from that of John or Paul?" This is easily explained, on the principle that when we wish a legal document written we choose a lawyer or a poetical article a poet, etc., so God when He wanted to speak in symbols chose an Ezekiel, a Daniel, a John, or in poetry a David. How are we to explain the fact that sometimes a New Testament writer in quoting from the Old Testament, instead of quoting literally paraphrases the quotation? For instance in Amos 9:11 we read: "In that day will I raise up the Tabernacle of David that is fallen and close up the breaches thereof and I will raise up his ruins and I will build it as in the days of old." But when the Apostle James in the First Church Council at Jerusalem, quotes this passage, he paraphrases it, saying— "After this I will return and will build again the Tabernacle of David which is fallen down and I will build again the ruins therefore and I will set it up." Acts.15:16. Why the change in the wording? Simply because the author of both passages was not Amos or James, but the Holy Spirit and an author has a perfect right to change the phraseology of a statement he may make in the first chapter of his book, in the tenth chapter, if by so doing, without contradicting himself, he can make his meaning clearer. That is an illuminating statement in I Pet. 1:11, where the Apostle tells us that it was the "Spirit of Christ" that testified through the Prophets of His "Suffering." That is, the "Spirit of Christ" took possession of the Prophets and through them forecast or prophesied His "Suffering" on the Cross, as in Isa. 53:1-12. The question is often asked, "Is there any difference between Bible Inspiration and the so-called inspiration of Poets, Orators, Preachers, and Writers of today? In answering the question the question we must distinguish between "Inspiration," "Revelation," and "Illumination." As we have seen "Bible Inspiration" is something totally different and unique from the inspiration of Poets, Writers and Public Speakers. It is an inspiration in which the Exact Words of God are imparted to the Speaker or Writer by the Holy Spirit. **"Bible Revelation,"** is the disclosure to men of things that they otherwise could never know, things hidden in the mind of God, such as His "Plan and Purpose in the Ages." "Bible Revelation " ceased with the Book of Revelation, there has been no new revelation from God since then, when men today claim that they have received some new revelation they must be classed as imposters. **"Spiritual Illumination"** is different from either Bible Inspiration or Revelation, it is the Work of the Holy Spirit in the Believer, by which he has his "Spiritual Understanding" opened to understand the Scriptures. John 16:12-15. The "Natural Man," cannot receive the things of the Spirit of God, neither can he know them, because they are Spiritually Discerned, I Cor. 2:11-14., The work then of the Holy Spirit in these days is not to impart some new revelation to men, or to inspire them to write or speak as the Prophets and Apostle of old, but to so illuminate men's minds and open up their understanding of the Scriptures that their heart will burn within them as they compare Scripture with Scripture and have revealed to them God's Plan and Purpose in the Ages as disclosed in His Holy Word. ***PRE–MILLENNIALISM.,*** The time of the Second Coming of Christ is the key that unlocks all "Truths" the vast majority of Christians believe in the personal return of the Lord, but they differ as to the time.

The Battle of the Culture

They are divided into two schools, the "pre– millennialists and the post-millennialists," the pre-millennialist believe that Christ will return before the millennium, the post-millennialists, that He will not come until after. By the Millennium is meant the period of 1000 years mentioned in Rev. 20:17, it is a common, but wholly erroneous impression, that pre– millennialists base their belief mainly, if not solely on this passage in the Apocalypse, the fact is, the question of whether Christ's return will precede or follow the Millennium antedates the Apocalypse. The Old Testament prophets in plain language and in glowing terms, foretold an era or age of universal righteousness and peace on this earth, under the reign of Messiah the Prince. That the disciples were not mistaken in their belief in such an Earthly Kingdom, ruled over by their promised Messiah, is evident from the fact that Jesus never reproved them for holding such a belief and after His resurrection and previous to His Ascension when they asked Him if He would "at that time restore the Kingdom of Israel" (Acts 1:6). He did not say—" You are mistaken in your area of an Earthly Kingdom, the Kingdom I came to set up and that was meant by the prophets, is a 'Spiritual Kingdom,' but He said— "It is not for you to know the "Times and Seasons". That is, when it shall be set up, the whole teaching of the Old Testament as to the "Coming of the Messiah" is Pre-Millennial. The only use that Premillennialites have for the "Thousand Year" passage in Rev.20:1-7 is to fix the length of that "Age of Righteousness and Peace." In fact Jewish tradition, based on the "Sabbatic Rest" of Gen. 2:1-3, taught that the "Seventh Thousand Years" from Creation was to be a period of "Sabbatic Rest," or what we call the Millennium. The passage in Revelation simply confirms this tradition, expunge the passage and you do not weaken the argument; you only leave as uncertain the length time that Age shall last. The Apostolic Church was Pre-Millennial and for over 200 years no other view was entertained, the writings of the "Church Fathers" abound in evidence of the fact. But about A.D. 250, Origen, one of the Church Fathers, conceived the idea that the words of scripture were but husk in which was hid the kernel of scripture truth, at once he began to "Allegorize" and "Spiritualize" the Scriptures, and thus founded that school of "Allegorizing" and "Spiritualizing" interpreters of Scripture, from which the Church and the Bible have suffered so much. The result was that the Church largely ceased to look for the Lord to return and set up an earthly kingdom, When Constantine became sole Emperor of Rome in A.D. 323, being favorable to Christianity, he united Church and State. A new difficulty now arose in the interpretation of scripture, if as was at that time believed, Rome was to be the seat of the Antichrist, the question arose or rather was suspiciously whispered— "is Constantine the Antichrist? Such a notion was unpalatable to the Roman Emperor and so a convenient explanation was discovered and adopted, that Antichrist was "Pagan Rome," and that the Millennium commenced when Constantine ascended the throne. This was given color by the great gifts and privileges bestowed on the Church by Constantine and led to the claim that the millennial blessings of the Old Testament had been transferred from the Jews to the Christian Church. But the claim that the Papal Church was the Antichrist would not down, when it was found impossible to expunge the Book of Revelation from the sacred canon, it was decided to lock up the scriptures and the Bible became a sealed book and the gloom of night settled down upon all Christendom. The result was the "Dark Ages" But amid the gloom God was not without witnesses to the truth. The Paulicians, Albigeneses, Waldenses, and other sects, bore testimony to the Premilliennial return of the Lord. But the darkness was not eternal, when the fullness of time was come the "Morning Star" of the Reformation, John Wycliffe, arose, and was soon followed by the "Sun," Martin Luther, the brightness of whose light dispelled the darkness. The doctrine of the Premillennial return of the Lord was revived but the Reformers did not go far enough, the period was one of religious strife and the formation of new religious sects, the result was an ebb of Spirituality and the growth of Rationalism, which refused to believe that the world was fast ripening for judgment and a new interpretation of the Millennial Reign of Christ was demanded.

The Battle of the Culture

This interpretation was furnished by the Rev. Daniel Whitby (1638-1726), a clergyman of the Church of England, who claimed that in reading the promises made to the Jews in the Old Testament of their restoration as a nation and the re-establishment of the Throne of David, he was led to see that these promises were spiritual and applied to the Church. This view he called a "New Hypothesis," He claimed that Israel and Mount Zion represented the Church, that the promised submission of the Gentiles to the Jews was simply prophetic of the conversion of the Gentiles and their entrance into the Church. That the lying down of the lion and the lamb together typified the reconciliation of the Old and New natures and that the establishment of an outward and visible kingdom at Jerusalem, over which Christ and the saints should reign was gross and carnal and contrary reason as it implied the mingling together of human and spiritual beings on earth. His "New Hypothesis" was that by the preaching of the Gospel Mohammedanism would be overthrown, the Jews converted, the Papal Church with the Pope (Antichrist) would be destroyed and there would follow a 1000 years of righteousness and peace known as the Millennium; at the close of which there would be a short period of Apostasy, ending in the return of Christ. There would then be a general resurrection of the dead, followed by a general judgment, the earth would be destroyed by fire and eternity would begin. The times were favorable for the "New Theory," A reaction had set in from the open infidelity of those days, all England was in a religious fervor, the "Great Awakening" followed under Whitefield and Wesley and it looked as Whitby claimed, that the millennium was about to be ushered in. That he was mistaken the events of history since that time have shown, it is evident that we are not in the Millennium now, nevertheless his "Theory" was favorably received everywhere and spread with great rapidity and became an established doctrine of the Church and is what is known today as the "Post-Millennial View of the second Coming of Christ and supposed to be the orthodox faith of the Church. In short, "Post-Millennialism" as advocated in our day is barely 350 years old while "Pre-Millennialism dates back to the days of Isaiah and Daniel.

QUESTIONING GOD

The sad thing is that this "false doctrine" of "Post-Millennialism" is taught in our Bibles by the headings of the chapters in the Old Testament, for illustration the headings of chapter forty-three and four of Isaiah reads— "The Lord comforted the Church with His promises, whereas the chapters are not addressed to the Church at all but to Jacob and Israel as we see by reading them. The ordinary reader overlooks the fact that the chapter headings of the Bible are put there by the publisher and should be omitted as they are misleading as for illustration the title to the Book of Revelation, which is called— "The Revelation of St John the Divine," in some version of the Bible, whereas it should be called "the Revelation of Jesus Christ," by which many of today's version do speak to what it should be. Rev.1:1, Premillennialists are divided into three "Schools of Interpretations," which are fundamentally antagonistic, known as "Pre-theorist, Historical and "Futurist" Schools. The Preterist School originated with the Jesuit Alcazer, His view was first put forth as a complete scheme in his work on the Apocalypse, published in A.D. 1614, it limits the scope of the Apocalypse to the events of the Apostle John's life and affirms that the whole prophecy was fulfilled in the destruction of Jerusalem by Titus and the subsequent fall of the persecuting Roman Empire, thus making the Empire Nero the "Antichrist." The purpose of scheme was transparent, it was to relieve the Papal Church from the stigma of being called the "Harlot Church" and the Pope from being called the "Antichrist," it is a view that is now but little advocated, the "Historical School," sometimes spoken of as the "President" scheme, interprets the Apocalypse as a series of prophesies predicting the events that were to happen in the world and in Church from John's day to end of time. The Revelation as referring to certain historical events that have and are happening in the world, they claim that "Antichrist" is a "System" rather than a "Person," and is represented by the Harlot Church of Rome. They interpret the "Time Element" in the book on the "Year Day Scale," this School has had some very able and ingenious advocates, this view, like the preceding was unknown to the early church.

The Battle of the Culture

It appeared about the middle of the Twelfth Century and was systematized in the beginning of the Thirteenth Century by the Abbot Joachim. Subsequently it was adopted and applied to the Pope by the forerunners and leaders of the Reformation and may be said to have reached its zenith in Mr. Ellicott's "Horae Apocalyptcae." It is frequently called the Prostestant interpretation because it regards Popery as exhausting all that has been predicted of the Antichristian power, it was a powerful and formidable weapon in the hands of the leaders of the Reformation and the conviction of its truthfulness nerved them to "love not their lives unto the death." It was the secret of the martyr heroism of Sixteenth Century, the "Futurist School" interprets the language of the Apocalypse "literally," except such symbols as are named as such and holds that the whole of the Book, from the end of the third chapter, is yet "future" and unfulfilled and that the greater part of the Book from the beginning of chapter six to the end of chapter nineteen, describes what shall come to pass during the last week of Daniel's Seventy Weeks." This view, while it dates in modern times only from the close of the Sixteenth Century, is really the most ancient of the three, it was held in many of its prominent features by the primitive Fathers of the Church and is one of the early interpretations of scripture truth that sunk into oblivion with the growth of Papacy and that has been restored to the Church in these last times. In its present form it may be said to have originated at the end of the Sixteenth Century, with the Jesuit Ribera, who, actuated by the same motive as the Jesuit Alcazar, sought to rid the Papacy of the stigma of being called the "Antichrist" and so referred the prophecies of the Apocalypse to the distant future. This view was accepted by the Roman Catholic Church and was for a long time confined to it, but strange to say, it has wonderfully revived since the beginning of the Nineteenth Century and that among Protestants, it is the most largely accepted of the three views. It has been charged with ignoring the Papal and Mohammedan systems, but this is far from the truth, for it looks upon them as fore-shadowed in the scriptures and sees in them the "Type" of those great "Anti-Types," yet future, the "Beast" and the "False Prophet."

QUESTIONING GOD

The "Futurist" interpretation of scripture is the one employed in this book, the Second and Premillennial Coming of Christ is the "Key" to the Scriptures, all of the prophetical writings makes it their terminal end. This is a dark world and the "Sure word of Prophecy" is given as a light to show us the way over the stormy sea of time, 2Pet. 1:19, Prophecy is not a haphazard guess, like our weather probabilities, it is History Written in Advance. The moment we grasp this idea of prophecy and clearly see the relation of Christ's Premillennial Coming to scripture truth, the Bible becomes a new book and doctrinal and prophetical truth, the Bible into their proper place and our theological system is no longer a chaos but an orderly plan.

MOUNTAIN PEAKS OF PROPHECY.,

The Bible is unlike all other "sacred books" in it bases its "Authenticity" and "Authority" on Prophecy, all other "sacred books" contain no predictions as to the future, it their authors had attempted to foretell future events, their non-fulfillment would, long ere this, have discredited their writings. Fulfilled prophecy is stronger evidence for the "Inspiration" and "Authenticity" of the Scriptures than miracles, prophecy is not a "haphazard guess," nor a "probability" made up on uncertain data like our "Weather Probabilities." Prophecy is "History Written in Advance," or, as another has said— "Prophecy is the mold of History" the importance of the study of the Prophetic Scriptures is seen when we recall that two-thirds of the Scriptures are Prophetic, either in type, symbol, or direct statement and more than one-half of the Old Testament prophecies and nearly all of the New Testament point to events yet future. Then this is a "Dark World," and men need the "Sure word of Prophecy" to Light them over the stormy "Sea of Time," 2 Pet. 1:19; when men see that God has a "Plan and Purpose" in the "Age" they take heart and have something to pin their faith to. It was because the religious leaders of Christ's day were not students of the Prophetic Scriptures that they failed to recognize Him when He came and if the religious leaders of our day despise and reject the study of Prophecy, they will not be ready for Christ's Second Coming.

The Battle of the Culture

There are "Four Prophetic Periods" clearly outlined in the Scriptures, **1.) PATRIARCHAL—B.C. 1921-1491, 2.) MOSAIC—B.C. 1921-1340, 3.) JEWISH—Post-Exilic— B.C. 500-400   Exilic—B.C. 600-500 Pre-Exilic—B.C. 900-600 (400 Years of Silence) 4.) APOSTOLIC—A.D. 27-100,** these prophecies divide themselves into three grand divisions: **1. PAST—** Fulfilled Prophecy, **2. PRESENT—** Fulfilling Prophecy, these are the prophecies that refer to the Jews, the Nations and the moral and religious character of the times   **3. FUTURE—** Unfulfilled Prophecy, the "Requirements" of a Genuine Prediction are five in number: 1. It must have been made known Prior to its fulfillment. 2. It must be beyond all Human Foresight. 3. It must give Details 4. A sufficient time must elapse between its publication and fulfillment to exclude the prophet or any interested party from fulfilling it. 5. There must be a clear and evident fulfillment of the prophecy is evident when we study the Law of "Compound Probabilities." If I were to predict an earthquake in Philadelphia next year the chance would be 1 in 2 that it would occur, if I should add another prediction, that it would be on the Fourth of July the chance is decreased to 1 in 4. And if add another detail that it will be in the daytime the chance then becomes 1 in 8, and if I should add a fourth detail the chance the chance would be 1-32, and if the details were 10 in number the chance would be 1 in 1024. Now there were 25 specific predictions made by the Old Testament Prophets bearing on the betrayal, trial, death and burial of Jesus, these were uttered by different prophets during the period from B.C. 1000 to B.C. 500, yet they were all literally fulfilled in 24 hours in one person. According to the law of "Compound Probabilities" there was one chance in 33,554,432 that these 25 predictions would be fulfilled as prophesied. If one prophet should make several predictions as to someone event, he might by collusion with others bring it to pass, but when a number of prophets, distributed over several centuries, give detailed and specific predictions age of to some event, the charge of collusion cannot be sustained.

QUESTIONING GOD

It is a fact that there were 109 predictions literally fulfilled at Christ's First Advent in the flesh, apply the Law of "Compound Probabilities" to this number and the chance was only one in Billions that they would be fulfilled in one person. The argument that Jesus employed to convince those two mourning disciples walking to Emmaus that He was "The Messiah," was the appeal to "Prophecy." "And beginning at Moses and all the Prophets, He expounded unto them in All the Scriptures (O.T. Scriptures), the things concerning Himself," Luke 24:27; It would be intensely interesting reading and amazingly helpful if we only had in Luke's Gospel a full report of that afternoon's conversation. The two disciples were familiar with the things that had occurred the previous week at the arrest, trial, crucifixion and burial of Jesus as well as the rumors of His resurrection. It was not difficult therefore for Jesus to take those things and by quoting from the Old Testament Scriptures show that they were just what the prophets had foretold would happen to the Messiah when He came. He reminded them that the prophets had said that the Messiah should be sold for 30 pieces of silver (Zech. 11:12), be betrayed by a friend (Psa. 41:9), forsaken by His disciples (Zech 13:7), accused by false witnesses (Psa. 35:11), be dumb before His accusers (Isa. 53:7), be scourged (Isa. 50:6), His garments parted (Psa. 22:18), mocked by His enemies (Psa. 22:7-8), be given gall and vinegar to drink (69:21), not a bone of His body broken (Psa. 34:20), die with male-factors (Isa. 53:12), that the price of His betrayal should be used to purchase a "Potter's Field" (Zech. 11:13), and that He should be buried in a rich man's tomb. Isa. 53:9. But Jesus doubtless did not stop with simply proving that the crucified Christ fulfilled all the requirements of prophecy, it was a long walk they had, Jesus doubtless joined them soon after they left Jerusalem for Emmaus, which was some 6 miles away and so had ample time in which to outline the "Prophetic Portrait" of the Messiah. Turning to Gen. 22:7-8, He pictured Isaac as a "Type" of Christ and that God spared Abraham's son, but did not spare His own Son, he then called attention to the institution of "The Pass-over," and recalled the fact that in preparing the lamb for roasting, two spits were used, one thrust lengthwise through the body for support over the fire and the other across the shoulders for turning, thus symbolizing the Cross on which the Lamb of God was suspended. He then reminded them that Jesus ha d said in one of His discourse— "And I, if I be Lifted Up, will draw all men unto me," John 12:32; and having thus refreshed their memory, He took them back to that incident in the history of the Children of Israel of "The Brazen Serpent," and pointed out that, that was type of how Jesus by being lifted up took the place of the "Brazen Serpent," and that all that look to Him in fait shall be delivered from the results of sin. Then Jesus spoke of the Prophet Jonah and what befell him and recalled His own prophecy, which doubtless they had heard but had forgotten, that— "As Jonah was three days and three nights in the whale's belly, so shall the Son of Man be three days and three nights in the heart of the earth" (Matt. 12:40), thus showing them that they should not have been surprised at the report they had heard that morning, that Jesus had Risen from the Dead. Is it any wonder that as Jesus thus went on outlining the "Prophetic Christ" and comparing Him with the "Historic Christ" they had known and loved that their heart "Burned within them" as He talked with them by the way and opened up to them the Scriptures. Luke 24:32. How easy a conundrum seems when we know the answer and how simple the Scriptures become when we see Christ in them, for "the Testimony of Jesus" is the "Spirit of Prophecy." Rev. 19:10. That is, the Spirit and purpose of all Prophecy is to testify of Jesus, how important then is the study of Prophecy, now we have seen that there were 109 predictions of the Old Testament Prophets literally fulfilled at Christ's First Advent, but there are 845 quotations from the Old Testament in the New Testament and 333 of these refer to Christ. They vary from types and figures that seem meaningless unless you place Christ in them, to exact predictions that at times descend to the minutest details, the only books of the Old Testament not quoted in the New Testament are Ruth, Ezra, Nehemiah, Songs of Solomon and Obadiah.

QUESTIONING GOD

The Old Testament Scriptures bear a "double witness" to Jesus, they point out both His "First" and "Second" Comings, and the same Prophet in referring to the "Two Comings" did not always name them in the proper order. This was confusing to the Bible students and religious leaders of Christ's day, in fact they did not know that there were to be "Two Comings," therefore they are not to be too harshly judged because they rejected Christ, because He did not at once set up an "Earthly Kingdom," they did not separate the prophecies that foretold His "Sufferings" from the prophecies that foretold His "Glory." 1 Pet. 1:10-12. They believed that all the prophecies that referred to the Messiah (Christ) were to be fulfilled at His First Coming, this accounts for why the people of Christ's day looked for Him to set up an Earthly Kingdom. They did not see that this "Present Dispensation," or "Church Age," was to intervene between the "Sufferings" (the Cross) and the "Glory" (the Crown), But we stand on this side of Calvary and can readily separate the fulfilled prophecies of the "First Advent" from the unfulfilled prophecies of the "Second Advent The Old Testament prophet saw the future as peaks of one mountain, He did not see that these peaks assembled themselves in groups, with a valley, the "VALLEY OF THE CHURCH," between, in the first group is the "Birth of Jesus," "Calvary," and "Pentecost." In the second group is "Antichrist," the "Revelation of Christ," and the "Kingship of Christ," The Prophet Isaiah (Isa. 61:1-2) did not see that "comma" in the second verse, that separated between the statements— "The acceptable Branch," and the "King who shall Reign and Prosper." The Prophets saw the "Prophetic" and "Kingly" work of Christ, but they did not see the "Priestly," they saw the "Altar" (Sacrificial), and the "Throne," but they did not see the "Table" (the Lord's Table) that was to come in between. The Prophet saw in a direct line along the "Peaks of Prophecy" and did not see the "valley" of "The Church" in between, our viewpoint is from the side we face the "Valley" with the "First Advent" (the Cross) to our left and the "Second Advent" (the Crown) to our right. All we have to do is to separate the prophecies of the "First Advent" from the prophetic reference to Christ in the Old Testament and apply the balance to His "Second Advent," this simplifies the study of Prophecy.

The Battle of the Culture

Isaiah's prophecies have mainly to do with the Messiah and Israel, Jeremiah is the Prophet of Israel's return to their own land Ezekiel has to do with the Restoration of Israel to their own land and with the Millennial Land, Restored Temple and the form of Worship. Daniel is the Prophet of the Gentiles and their final great events that shall happen at the Second Coming of Christ, as— 1. Antichrist (Idol Shepherd), Zech. 11:15-17. 2. Armageddon Zech. 14:1-3. 3. Conversion of Israel, Zech. 12:9-14. 4. Christ's Return to Olivet, Zech. 14:4-11. 5. Old Age in Jerusalem, Zech. 8:3-8 6. Feast of Tabernacles 14:16-21. Notice that Zechariah does not see these events in their chronological order, all the Major Prophets and 9 of the Minor Prophets emphasize the "Kingship of Christ," and it was this that confused the Religious Leaders of Christ's day. The Perspective of Prophecy of the prophets foresaw the future events from the Birth of Christ on down to the New Heavens and the New Earth, a careful study will show that the Prophet Nahum saw beyond his time, while the Prophet Isaiah saw more and the farthest of all the prophets.

The Second Coming of Christ

there is fact in history more clearly established than the fact of the "First Coming" of Christ, but as His "First Coming," it is evident that there must be another "Coming" to completely fulfill them. It was because the religious leaders of Christ's day failed to distinguish between the prophecies that related to His "First Coming," and those that related to His "Second Coming" that they rejected Him. Peter tells us (1 Pet. 1:10-11) that the prophets themselves did not clearly perceive the difference between the "Sufferings" and "Glory" of Christ. That is, they did not see that there was a "Time Space" between the "Cross" and the "Crown," and that the "Cross" would precede the "Crown." But we have no such excuse, we live on this side of the "Cross," and we can readily pick out all the remainder to His "Second Coming," it is clear then that Christ's "First Coming," important as it was, is not the "doctrinal centre" of the Scriptures, that is, Christ's First Coming was not the centre of a circle that contains all doctrine but was one of the foci of an ellipse of which the other is the "Second Coming."

QUESTIONING GOD

The whole Mediatorial Work of Christ, Prophetic, and Priestly and kingly, this is included in an ellipse, the foci of which are the "First" and "Second" Comings of Christ. The "Cross" represents His "First Comings" and the "Crown" His Second Comings. Between the "Fall" and the "First Coming" we have the "Altar," which points backward to the "Fall" and forward to the "Cross," between the "Coming" we have the "Table" which points backward to the "Cross" and forward to the "Second Coming." Between the "Second Coming" and the surrendering of the "Kingdom," the Apostle Paul in his epistles clearly distinguishes between the "Comings" and their doctrinal significance, in his letter to the Hebrew's he classifies Christ's "appearing" as "Hath He appeared" (Heb. 9:26), "Now to appear" (Heb. 9:24), "Shall He appear" (Heb. 9:28). In his letter to Titus (Titus 2:11-12), he brings out the doctrinal significance of these "appearing," as a Prophet He died for our "Justification," as a Priest He lives at the right hand of God not only as our Advocate, but our "Glorification." While the First and Second Comings of Christ are separated by this Dispensation they are nevertheless not complete in themselves, the Second necessitated the First and the First demands the Second, they are both necessary to complete the Plan of Salvation. The First Coming was for the salvation of my "Soul" the Second is for the salvation of my "Body," for there can be no resurrection of the body until Christ comes back. The Second Coming as to the fact, 1. **The Testimony of Jesus Himself., Matt 16:27, "For the Son of Man shall come in the Glory of His Father, with His Angels and then He shall reward every man according to His work. Matt 25:31-32., "When the Son of Man shall come in His glory and all the holy angels with Him, then shall He sit upon the Throne of His Glory and before Him shall be gathered all nations and Ne shall separate them one from another, as a shepherd divided his sheep from the goats." John 14:2-3., "In my Father's house are many mansions; if it were not so I would have told you, I go to prepare a place for you, and if I go and prepare a place for you I will come again and receive you unto myself; that where I am there ye may be also." John 21:22, "If I will that he tarry till I come what is that to thee? Follow thou me."**

2. The Testimony of the Heavenly Beings., Acts 1:10-11., "and while they looked steadfastly toward heaven as he went up, behold, two men stood by them in white apparel; which also said Men of Galilee," why do you stand here looking into the sky? This same Jesus, who has been taken from you into heaven, will come back in the same way you seen him go into heaven. This passage declares that the same Jesus shall return in like manner as He went that is, that His return will be visible and personal, the two "men" that "stood by" were probably Moses and Elijah. They appeared with Jesus on the Mount of Transfiguration, they were doubtless the "two men" who testified to the woman at the tomb that Jesus had risen (Luke 24:4-5) and they will be the "Two Witness" that shall testify during the Tribulation. Rev.11:3-12.

3. The Testimony of the Apostles., Paul— "For our conversation is in heaven; from whence also we look for the Savior, the Lord Jesus Christ: who shall change our vile body, that it may be fashioned like unto his glorious body, according to the working whereby he is able even to subdue all things unto himself." Phil. 3:20-21. "Looking for that Blessed Hope and the Glorious Appearing of God and our Savior Jesus Christ." Titus 2:13. So Christ was once offered to bear the sins of many and unto them that look for him shall he appear the second Time without sin unto salvation." Heb. 9:28.

James— " Be patient therefore, brethren, unto the coming of the Lord," James 5:7., **Peter**— " for we have not followed cunningly devised fables when we made known unto you the power and coming of our Lord Jesus Christ but were eye-witnesses of majesty." 2 Pet. 1:16. Peter here refers to the Transfiguration of Christ on the Mount (Matt. 17:1-5), which was a type of His Second Coming, Moses was a type of the resurrection saints, and Elijah of those who shall be translated without dying. Peter, James and John were a type of the Jewish Remnant that shall see Him when He comes and the remaining disciples at the foot of the mount, unable to cast the demon out of the boy, of those professed followers of Jesus who shall be left behind at the Rapture and who shall be powerless to cast the demons out of the demon-possessed people of that period.

Jude— " And Enoch also, the seventh from Adam, prophesied of these, saying, Behold, the Lord cometh with ten thousand of his saints, to execute judgment upon all and to convince all that are ungodly among them of all their ungodly deeds which they have ungodly committed and of all their hard speeches which ungodly sinners have spoke against him." Jude 14-15.   **John—** "And now, little children, abide in him; that, when he shall appear, we may have confidence and not be ashamed before him at his coming 1 John 2:28. "Behold, he cometh with clouds and every eye shall see him and they also which pierced him and all kindred's of the earth shall wail because of him even so, Amen." Rev. 1:7 **4. The Testimony of the Lord's Supper.,** For as often as ye eat this bread and drink this cup, ye do show the Lord's death till He come," 1 Cor. 11:26, the Lord's Supper is not a permanent ordinance, it will be discontinued when the Lord returns, it is Memorial Feast, it looks back to the Cross and forward to the "Coming." An engagement ring is not intended to be permanent; it is simply a pledge of mutual love and loyalty and gives place to the wedding ring. So the Lord's Table may be looked upon as a betrothal pledge left to the Church during the absence of her betrothed, Paul in all his epistles refers but 13 times to Baptism, while he speaks of the Lord's return 50 times. One verse in every 30 in the New Testament refers to Christ Second Coming; there are 20 times as many references in the Old Testament to Christ's Second Coming as to His First Coming. **The Five Theories.,** while the majority of professing Christians admit the fact of the Second Coming of Christ, they are not agreed as to the "manner" or "time," there are five theories as to the Second Coming. **1.That His coming again is Spiritual and was fulfilled at Pentecost,** it was not Christ but the Holy Spirit that came at Pentecost and his coming was conditioned on Christ's absence, for Jesus said, It is expedient for you that I go away; for if I go not away, the Comforter (H.S.) will not come unto you; but I depart, I will send Him unto you," John 16:7, If the Holy Spirit is only another manifestation of Christ, then they are identical and that nullifies the Trinity.

The Battle of the Culture

The fact is, the whole New Testament was written after Pentecost and declares over 150 times that the Second Coming of Christ was still future and more, none of the events predicted as accompanying the Second Coming occurred at Pentecost, such as the Resurrection of the "Dead in Christ," the Translation of the "Living Saints," the Binding of Satan," etc. **2. That the Conversion of the sinner is the Coming of the Lord.** This cannot be, for at conversion the sinner comes to Christ, not Christ to the sinner and the sinner's conversion is the work of the Holy Spirit and the sinner's conversion is the work of the Holy Spirit and not the work of Christ. It is true that there is such a thing as the spiritual indwelling of Christ in the believer but His Second Coming, Like His First Coming is to be an outward, visible personal coming. **3. That death is the Coming of the Lord.**, the text that is used more than any other for funeral sermons is— " Watch, therefore; for ye know neither the day nor the hour where in the Son of Man cometh," Matt. 25:13, The context shows that this refers to a future coming of Christ, Christ could not come to the earth every time a person dies for two reasons— (1) A soul passes into eternity every second this would necessitate Christ's remaining continuously on the earth. (2) Christ is engaged in His High Priestly functions in the Heavenlies and could not leave them to come to the earth for the souls of the dying. The fact is that at death the believer goes to Christ, Christ does not come for him; death is always spoken of as a departure. "Absent from the body, present (at home) with the Lord," 2 Cor. 5:6-8, if Jesus had meant by His Second Coming "Death," he would have said to His Disciples— " If I go and prepare a place for you, I will send Death to bring you to myself," but He did not. He said— "I will come again and receive you unto myself," the last chapter of John's Gospel settles the matter, Peter said to Jesus— "Lord and what shall this man (referring to John) do? Jesus said— "If I want him to remain alive until I return, what is that to you? You must follow me," Because of this, the rumor spread among the believers that this disciple would not die, but Jesus did not say that he would not die; he only said, If I want him to remain alive until I return, what is that to you? John. 21:21-23.

We see from this that the Disciples did not think that "Coming of the Lord" meant "death." There was a great difference between these two things in their mind, death is an enemy (1 Cor. 15:26, 55), it holds us in the grave, it robs the body of its attractiveness, it is the Wages of Sin (Rom. 6:23) and the result of God's wrath, while the Second Coming of Christ is a manifestation of His love. Christ is the "Prince of Life," there can be no death where He is, He is the "Resurrection" and the "Life," and when He Comes, He will change our vile body, that it may be fashioned like unto His "Glorious Body." Phil. 3:20-21. **4. That the "Destruction of Jerusalem" in A.D. 70 by the Romans was Second Coming of the Lord.** The Lord was not present at the destruction of Jerusalem, it was destroyed by Roman soldiers, and none of the things that are to occur at the "Second Coming" occurred at the destruction of Jerusalem, such as the resurrection of the dead, the translation of the living saints and the physical changes that are to occur at Jerusalem and in the land of Palestine at Christ's coming. Zech. 14:4-11, Ez. 47:1-12., Christ's purpose in coming back is not to destroy Jerusalem, but to Restore it. It must be trodden down of the Gentile until the "Time of the Gentiles" are fulfilled, then shall they see the Son of Man coming in a cloud with power and great glory," Luke 21:24-28. The Book of Revelation, written 26 years after the destruction of Jerusalem, speaks of the Second Coming of Christ as still future **5. That the "Diffusion of Christianity" is the Second Coming of the Lord.**, this cannot be true, for the "Diffusion of Christianity" is gradual whereas the Scriptures declare that the "Return of the Lord" shall be sudden and unexpected, as a "Thief in the Night," Matt. 24:27, 36, 42, 44. 1 Thess.5:2, Rev. 3:3. Again the "Diffusion of Christianity" is a process, while the Scriptures invariably speak of the "Return of the Lord" as an event, the diffusion of Christianity brings salvation to the wicked, whereas the "Return of the Lord" is said to bring not salvation but sudden Destruction, 1 Thess. 5:2-3; 2 Thess. 1:7-10. **II. As to the Time,** of the exact time we cannot be certain, when Jesus was on the earth He said— "But of that day and that hour knows no man, no, not the angels which are in heaven, neither (not yet) the Son, but the Father."

The Battle of the Culture

Mark 13:32. After His Resurrection and before His Ascension, He refused to satisfy the curiosity of His Disciples, saying to them— "It is not for you to know times or the seasons which the Father has put in His own power." Acts.1:7. Jesus knew of Daniel's Prophecy of the Seventy Weeks, (Dan. 9:20-27), but He fixed no dates for this fulfillment, the student of prophecy is not to be a "date-setter," but he is to watch. "Signs" are for the Jews," there is nothing to prevent Christ coming for His Church at any time, while we do not know the day or the hour of Christ's Coming we know that it will be **Pre-Millennial.**

By Pre-Millennial we mean before the Millennium, that is, before the period of a "Thousand Years" spoken of in Rev. 20:1-6. This period is spoken of in other scriptures as "The Kingdom," and is described in glowing terms by the prophets as a time when the earth shall be blessed with a universal rule of righteousness. The passage in Rev. 20:1-6 simply tells us that the length of the period shall be 1000years, the very structure of the New Testament demands that Christ shall return before the Millennium. Here are a few reasons. 1. When Christ comes He will raise the Dead, but the Righteous dead are to be raised before the Millennium that they may reign with Christ during the 1000years, hence there can be no Millennium before Christ comes. Rev 20:5. 2. When Christ comes He will separate the Tares from the Wheat, but as the Millennium is a period of Universal Righteousness the separation of Tares and Wheat must take place before the Millennium, therefore there can be no Millennium before Christ comes. Matt. 13:40-43. 3. When Christ comes Satan shall be bound, but as Satan is to be bound during the Millennium, there can be no Millennium until Christ comes. Rev.20:1-3. 4.When Christ comes Antichrist is to be destroyed, but as Antichrist is to be destroyed before the Millennium there can be no Millennium until Christ comes. 2 Thess. 2:8; Rev.19:20. 5. When Christ comes the Jews are to be restored to their own land, but as they are to be restored to their own land before the Millennium, there can be no Millennium before Christ comes. Ez. 36: 24-28; Rev.

QUESTIONING GOD

1:7; Zech. 12:10. 6. When Christ comes it will be unexpectedly, and we are commanded to watch lest He take us unawares. Now if He is not coming until after the Millennium, and the Millennium is not yet here, why command us to watch for an event that is over 1000 years off? **III. As to the Manner,** He will return in the same manner as He went, Acts 1:11., He went up Bodily and Visibly and He shall come in like manner, He went in a cloud, and He will return in a cloud, "Behold, He cometh with the clouds; and every eye shall see Him, and they also which pierced Him; and all kindreds of the shall wail because of Him." Rev. 1:7, the only difference will be that He went up alone, He will return as King (Luke 19:12), followed by a retinue of the angelic host. "For the Son of man shall come in the glory of his Father with His angels; and then and then He shall reward every man according to his works," Matt16:27, His return however will be in **Two Stages**. He will come first in the region of our atmosphere, and the dead in Christ, and the living saints shall be caught up to meet Him in the Air." Then after the risen and translated saints have been judged and rewarded for their works and they, as the Church, the Bride of Christ, have been married to Him, He will come with them to the earth and land on the Mount of Olives, the place from whence He ascended. "and His feet shall stand in that day upon the Mount of Olives, which is before Jerusalem on the east, and Mount of Olives shall cleave in the midst thereof toward the east and toward the west, and there shall be a very great valley; and half of mountain shall remove towards the north, and half of it toward the south." Zech. 14:4. The First Stage of His Return is called **"The Rapture;"** the Second Stage— **"The Revelation,"** The time between the two Stages is not less than seven years, and is occupied in the heavens by the **"Judgment of Believers for work,"** and on the earth by **"The Great Tribulation." First Stage—The Rapture,** The Rapture is described in Thess. 4:15-17, "For this we say unto by the word of the Lord, that we which are alive and remain unto the coming of the Lord shall not prevent them which are asleep. For the Lord Himself shall descend from heaven with a shout, with the voice of the Archangel (Michael) and with the trump of God and the Dead in Christ shall rise;

The Battle of the Culture

then we which are Alive and Remain (saints only) shall be caught up together with them in the clouds, to meet the Lord in the Air, and so shall we ever be with the Lord." From this we see that "The Rapture" will be twofold. 1. The Resurrection of the Dead in Christ. 2. The Translation of the "Living Saints." This twofold character of "The Rapture" Jesus revealed to Martha when He was about to raise her brother Lazarus. He said to her: "I am the Resurrection and the Life," he that believed in Me though he was dead yet shall he (First Resurrection Saints); and whosoever Lived (is alive when I come back) and believed in Me shall never Die." John 11:25-26. This twofold character of the Rapture, Paul emphasizes in his immortal chapter on the resurrection, "Behold, I show you a Mystery, we shall not all sleep, but we shall all be changed, in a moment, in the twinkling of an eye, at the last trump; for the trumpet shall sound, and the dead shall be raised and we shall be changed. For this Corruptible (the dead in Christ) must put on the incorruption, and this mortal (the living saints) must put on immortality, So when this corruptible shall have put on incorruption, and this mortal shall have put on immortality, then shall be brought to pass the saying that is written, Death is swallowed up in Victory. O Death, Where is your Sting? O Grave, where is your Victory?" 1 Cor. 15:51-57, the last two lines refer only to those who are "changed without dying," for it is only those who will not die who can shout— "O Death, Where is your Sting? O Grave, Where is your Victory?" In 2 Cor. 5:1-4. Paul expresses his longing, and the longing of the Saints, to be among those who should not be "unclothed" by Death, but who should be "clothed upon" by Immortality "Without Dying." " For we know that if our earthly house of this tabernacle (the body) were dissolved (that is die), we have a building of God, a house not made with hands, eternal in the heavens. For in this (body) we groan, earnestly desiring to be "clothed upon" with our house which is from heaven; if so be that being "clothed" we shall not be naked, for we that are in the tabernacle (the body) do groan, being burdened; not for that we would be unclothed (by death), but clothed upon (by immortality), that mortality might be swallowed up of life."

QUESTIONING GOD

In his letter to the Philippians, while Paul hopes that— "If by any means he may attain unto the (out from among the dead) Resurrection, yet he pressed toward the mark for the prize of the High (out and up) Calling of God in Christ Jesus." Phil. 3:11-14. That is, while Paul would esteem it a great thing to rise from the dead at the First Resurrection and be "Caught Up" with those who should be "changed," yet he would esteem it a "prize" if he could be caught up "without dying," that is, live until Jesus came back, the Rapture will be a "Surprise." "Therefore keep watch, because you do not know on what day your Lord will come, but understand this: If the owner of the house had known at what time of the night the thief was coming, he would have kept watch and would not have let his house be broken into. So you also must be ready, because the Son of Man will come at an hour when you do not expect him. Matt. 24:42-44. "Look, I come as a thief, blessed is the one who stays awake and remains clothed, so as not to go naked and be shamefully exposed." Rev. 16:15. "But of the times and the seasons, brethren, ye have no need that I write unto you. For yourselves know perfectly that the "Day of the Lord" (the day of His Return), so cometh as a thief in the night. For when they shall say, Peace and Safety; then sudden destruction cometh upon them as travail upon a woman with child, and they shall not escape." This refers to a Second Stage of Christ's Coming, the "Revelation," when He shall take vengeance upon His enemies. 2 Thess. 1:7-10. But Paul adds— "But you, brethren, are not in darkness, that the day would overtake you like a thief." 1 Thess. 5:1-4. We see from this that when Christ comes back it will be when we are not expecting Him. He will come as a thief comes, a thief does not announce his coming, and he comes for a certain purpose. He does not take everything there that is in the house, he take only the precious things, the jewels, the gold, the silver and fine wearing apparel, he does not come to stay, as soon as he secures what he is after he departs. So Jesus at the Rapture will come and take away the saints only, the thief leaves much more than he takes, he leaves the house and the furniture and the household utensils.

The Battle of the Culture

So the Lord at the Rapture will leave the wicked and the great mass of the heathen behind, for those who will be taken will be comparatively few, the rapture will be "Elective." It will not only separate the saints from unbelievers, but it will separate husbands from wives, brothers from sisters, friends from friends. "I tell you, in that night there shall be two men in one bed; the one shall be taken, and the other shall be left, two women shall be grinding together; the one shall be taken, and the other left. Two men shall be in the field; the one shall be taken, and the other left," Luke 17:34-36, the words "men" and "women" in the passage are in italics, that means that they are not in the original, and so the passage should read there shall be "Two in one Bed," husband and wife, or two brothers, or sisters, or two friends. Two in "bed" indicates night; two grinding at the mill, morning or evening; two in the field mid-noon, this shows that the Rapture will happen all over the earth at the same time or as the Apostle describes it in a "moment," or the "twinkling of eye." "As the lightning comes from the east and flashes even to the west, so will the coming of the Son of Man be, wherever the corpse is, there the vultures will gather. (Matt. 24: 27-28.)   This is the way Jesus puts it, and the "Rapture" will be the most startling "event" of this Age and Dispensation, as it is to occur in the twinkling of an eye and all over the earth at the same time, that part of the world that is not asleep will witness the event. As to the "Shout of the Lord," the Voice of the Archangel," and the "Trump of God" we do not know whether their sound will be heard and distinguished by others than the "dead in Christ" and the "living saints." We know that one day the Father spoke to Christ in a voice that He understood, but the people who stood by mistook it for "thunder." John 12:28-29. When the Lord appeared to Saul of Tarsus on the road to Damascus and spoke to him, the men that journeyed with him stood speechless, hearing a voice," but seeing no man, and not understanding what was said. Acts.9:3-7. We know however that the dead in Christ will hear the sound, for it will be "intensely penetrating," there will be no graves so deep, no catacombs so rock covered, no pyramids or mausoleums so thick, but what the sound shall reach their depths and the "dead in Christ" shall hear the cry— "awake you sleeping saints and arise from the dead, it is morning, the morning of the First Resurrection." On the morning of the glorious day the air filled with the "spirits" of the "Dead in Christ," come back to earth to get their bodies, raised and glorified. Whether the cemeteries and country church yards will look like ploughed fields, and monuments and grave slabs be overturned and vaults and places of sepultures be shattered by the exodus of those who found their last place there, and thus testify to the fact of the literal bodily resurrection of the dead, or whether the sainted dead shall slip out of their sepulchers without breaking the seal, the angel rolling away the stone simply to show that the tomb was empty, we are told, only the event itself will disclose the manner of the First Resurrection. If the dead slip out of their places of sepulture without disturbing them, the First Resurrection will be secret and probably unknown to the world, but it will not be so with the "Living Saints" who are translated. If it is night on our side of the globe when the Rapture occurs the community will wake up in the morning to find all the real Christians gone, disappeared in the night. Many may hear the sound of the "Midnight cry"— "Behold **the Bridegroom comes,**" but thinking it only thunder, will turn over for another nap, but in the morning they will find the bedroom door locked, with the key on the inside, just as they locked it before retiring, and the clothes of the loved one who occupied the room with them lying where they were placed when taken off the night before, but that loved one, who was a Christian, missing. Husbands will wake up to find that Christian wives are gone, and wives will wake up to find Christian husbands gone, Brothers and sisters will be missed, and dear children absent, and not an infant will be missed, and dear absent, and not an infant will be left behind. Many faithful servants and employees will not report for duty, and the world will awake to the fact that the Bible is true, and the much despised doctrine of the Pre-interpretation of scripture. If it be day with us when the Rapture occurs, the "Event" will be starting, as it was in the days of Noah (Matt. 24:36-39, the people will be eating and drinking, marrying and giving in marriage, buying and selling, planting and building.

The Battle of the Culture

If it be at a pleasant time of the year, the boats, and cars, and parks will be filled with pleasure seekers, if it be in the midst of the week, and during the business hours of the day, the shops and the streets of the cities lined with men , woman and children on pleasure and business bent. Suddenly a noise from heaven will be heard like a great peal of thunder, the people will rush to doors and windows, and those on the streets and in the fields will look up to see what has happened. To the vast majority it will be but a startling and alarming sound, and to many it will be the "Voice of the Lord." But when the people recover from their surprised and affrighted condition they will discover that a great many people are missing, and that the missing were the best people in the community, the large department Stores, Banking Institutions, Manufacturing plants, and other places of business will find their working force depleted by the loss of the faithful employees. People walking on the streets will find their companions gone, and the streets car lines will be blocked because of absent motormen, conductors and teamsters, railroads and cruise ship lines will be crippled, and confusion will reign everywhere. In many homes the servants will be missing and members of the family will come home to find loved ones gone. At first the whole thing will be a Mystery, until someone who had heard or read about the "Rapture of the Saints," realizing what has happened, will explain the situation. But one of the surprises of that day will be that so many professing Christians, and among them many ministers and Christian workers, will be left behind, while some who were not known to be Christians will be missing. The next day's paper will be full of what happen the day before, and many of them will be swelled to twice their ordinary size by the pressure on their advertising columns for information as to missing ones, and for help to fill important vacancies and positions of trust. For a few days the excitement will be intense, then the people will settle down to the inevitable , with the exception of a few who will repent and turn to God, the mass of the people will become more hardened and wicked than before, and some who lost loved ones will be embittered. As the Holy Spirit will have gone back with the Raptured Ones," and the "Saint," the Salt of the earth, been taken out, there will be nothing to prevented the rapid degeneration and all manner of crime and worldliness will increase and pave the way for the manifestation of Antichrist, under whose administration the world will rapidly ripen for judgment. Who are to be taken, some claim that "all" the Church are to be caught out before the Tribulation, while some claim that only the "Waiting" and "Watching" Saints shall be caught out before the Tribulation, and that the rest must pass through it. The latter base their claim on Heb. 9:28, where it says— "Unto them that look for Him shall He appear the Second time without sin unto salvation." While this might apply to the living when He appears, it certainly cannot apply to the dead there are tens and hundreds of thousands who "fell asleep in Jesus" who never heard of the Premillennial Coming of the Lord, or at least never grasped its meaning, and who therefore never "watched" and "waited" and "looked" for His Appearing. They surely are "In Christ" and the "Dead in Christ" are to rise at the Rapture, Paul does not say in 1 Thess. 4:16-17, that it will be the "dead" who "watched" and "waited" and "looked," and those who are "alive" and "watch" and "wait" and "look" for his appearing that shall be "caught out," but the dead "In Christ," and we who "Are Alive And Remain." Then there is another fact that we must not forget, and that is, the Unity of the Church, "For as the Body is One, and hath many members and all the Members of that One Body, Being Many, are One Body: so also is Christ, for by One Spirit are we all Baptized into one Body." 1 Cor. 12:12-13. All then who have been "born again" (John 3:3-7) are part of Christ's "Body," and we cannot conceive of Christ's "Body" being divided; part of it remaining "asleep" in the grave, and part of it "raised in glory;" part of it left to pass through the Tribulation, and part of it "changed" and caught up to meet Him in the air. If "all" the Church are to pass through the Tribulation, then instead of waiting and watching "for the Lord," we should be waiting and watching "for the Tribulation," which is contrary to the teaching of Christ Himself. Matt24:42-44.

The Battle of the Culture

The Tribulation is not for the perfecting "of the Saints," It has nothing to do with the Church, it is the time of Jacob's Trouble" (Jer. 30:7), and is the "Judgment of Israel," and it is God's purpose to keep the Church out of it. Rev. 3:10. The Book of Revelation is written in chronological order, after the fourth chapter the Church is seen no more upon the earth until she appears in the nineteenth chapter coming with the Bridegroom "from" Heaven. The entire time between these two chapters is filled with appalling judgments that fall upon those that "dwell on the earth," and as the Church is not of the earth, but is supposed to "sit together in Heavenly Places in "Christ Jesus" (Eph. 2:6), she will not be among those "dwell on the earth" in those days. The confusion is largely due to the fact that students of Prophetic Truth do not distinguish between Christ's coming for His Saints, and with His Saints, the former is called the "Rapture," the latter the "Revelation." Numerous passages in scripture speak of Christ coming "with" His Saints (Zech. 14:5, Col. 3:4, 1 Thess. 3:13, 1Thess.4:14, Jude 14), but it is evident that they cannot come with Him, if they had not been previously caught out to Him. All such passages refer therefore to the "Revelation" and "Rapture," the typical teaching of the Scriptures demand that the Church be caught out before the tribulation, Joseph was a type of Christ and he was espoused to, and married Asenath, a Gentile bride, during the time of his "rejection by his brethren," and "before the famine," which typified the Tribulation, because it was the time of "Judgment of the Brethren." This is the time of Christ's rejection by "His Brethren"— the Jews, and to complete the type He must get His Bride— the church, "before" the Tribulation. Moses, who is also a type of Christ, got his bride, and she a Gentile, after his rejection by his brethren, and "before" they passed through the Tribulation under Pharaoh. Ex. 2:23-25. Enoch, a type of the "Translation Saints," was caught out "before' the Flood, and the Flood is a type of the Tribulation, and Noah and his family of the "Jewish Remnant" or 144,000 sealed ones of Rev. 7:1-8, who will be preserved through the Tribulation. How thrilling the thought that some of us shall not die, that in a moment, in the "twinkling of an eye" without being unclothed by the ghastly hands of Death, and instead of the winding sheet of the grave, we shall be instantly changed and clothed with the glorious garments of immortality. What a transport of joy will fill our being as we suddenly feel the thrill of immortality throbbing through our veins, and find ourselves being transported through the air in the company of fellow Christians and of our loved ones who fell asleep in Jesus. What welcome recognitions and greetings there will be as we journey up with them to the "Bridal Halls of Heaven," where we shall join in the new and triumphal song of Moses and the Lamb. Rev.5:9-10. **Second Stage—the Revelation** at the "Second Stage" of Christ's Second Coming, the "Revelation," we shall behold His "Glory." When Jesus came the first time he was disguised in the flesh, the "Incarnation" was the hiding of His Power, the veiling of His Deity. Now and then gleams of the glory shot forth as on the Mt. of Transfiguration; but when he comes the Second Time we shall behold Him clothed with the glory He had with the Father before the world was. The "Revelation" will rise on that day strong and clear, Gentile breezes will breezes will waft themselves over the earth, there will be no signs of a storm or of the coming Judgment. The people will be buying and selling, building, planting, eating, drinking, marrying and giving in marriage, the statement will be revolving in their minds new plans for the world's betterment. The Philanthropic will be devising new ways to help the people, the pleasure-loving will be seeking new sources of pleasure, the wicked will be plotting dark deeds; and the unbelieving will be proving to their own satisfaction that there is no God, no Heaven, no Hell, no coming Judgment, when suddenly there will be a change in the distant Heaven there will appear a **"Point of Light,"** outshining the sun. It will be seen descending toward the earth, as it descends it will assume the form of a bright cloud out of which shall stream dazzling beams of light, and flashes of lightning, it will descend apace as if on wings of the whirlwind, and when it reaches its destination over the brow of the of the Mt. of Olives it will stop and unfold itself to the terrified and awestricken beholders, and there will be revealed to them Jesus seated on a "White Horse" (Rev. 19:11-16) and accompanied with His Saints and the armies of Heaven. Then shall appear the sign (a cloud) of the Son of Man in Heaven; and then shall all the tribes of the earth mourn, and they shall see the Son of Man coming in the clouds of Heaven with Power and Great Glory." Matt. 24:30. **The Immanency of the Second Coming,** one of the objections to the Doctrine of the Second Coming of Christ's is the claim that He may come back at any time, Post-millennialists tell us that the writers of the New Testament looked for Him to come back in their day, and that He did not do so, is proof that they were mistaken, and that Paul in his later writings modified his statements as to the immanency of Christ's return. It is a fact that while Jesus said: "Watch therefore: for ye know not what hour your Lord doth come... Therefore are ye also ready: for in such an hour as ye think not the Son of Man cometh" (Matt. 24:42-44), He intimated that His return would be delayed, as in the Parable of the Talents, where it is said: "After a long time the Lord of those servants cometh." Matt. 25:19. What Jesus wanted to teach was the sudden and unexpected character of His return, as to the Apostles, while they exhorted their followers to be ready, for the "night is far spent, the day is at hand," and the "coming of the Lord draws nigh," their language simply implied "immanency," but not necessarily immediateness. And the use of the word "We" in 1 Cor. 15:51, "We" shall not all sleep, but We shall all be changed," is not a declaration that the Lord would return in Paul's day and some would not die but be translated, for the Apostle is talking about the Rapture and he means by "We" a certain class of persons the saints that shall be alive when that event occurs, whether in his day or at some time. It was clearly known to our Lord that certain events must come to pass before His Return, but to have disclosed that fact would have nullified the command to "Watch," therefore He in "mystery form," as in the seven parables of Matt. 13, hid the fact that His Return would be delayed. It would take for the "Sowing of the Seed," the growth of the "Wheat" and "Tares," the growth of the "Mustard Tree," and the "Leaving of the Meal,"

QUESTIONING GOD

So rapid was the spread of the Gospel in the first century that the followers of Christ were warranted in looking for the speedy return of the Lord, but it was true then, as in every century since, that we do not know what the extent of the "Harvest" is to be, and when it will ripe, so the Lord can return. Matt. 13:30. Uncertainty then as to the "time" of the lord's Return is necessary to promote the watchful spirit, if the early Church had known that the Lord's Return would have been delayed for 20 centuries, the incentive to watchfulness would have been wanting. By "Immanency" we mean "may happen at any time," for illustration you hurry to the railroad station to catch a train, you find the train has not arrived, though it is past the hour, though it is late it is on the way, and it would not be safe for you to leave the situation, for it may arrive any minute, but as a matter of fact, it does not come for half an hour. Now if you had known that it would not arrive for an half an hour you would have used the time in some other way than "waiting" and "watching," So we see that "Immanency" does not necessarily imply "Immediateness," but does demand "watchfulness". It is the firm conviction of the writer that there has been unnecessary delay in the Return of the Lord, caused by failure of the Church to obey the "Divine Commission" to evangelize the world (Matt. 28:19-20), and it is past the time when He should have returned, Of course, this was foreseen by God, and His foreknowledge has held back the development of the forces of evil, etc., until the "Fullness of Gentiles" should be gathered in, and the "Harvest" is ripe for the gathering. Rev.14:14-20, at no time in the history of the Christian Church have the conditions necessary to the Lord's Return been so completely fulfilled as at the present time; therefore, His Coming is Imminent, and will not probably be long delayed, Let us be ready and watching. While the writer, as stated, is disposed to believe that Return of the Lord is past due, and while he is no time setter, yet there is a "theory" that throw some light on the Immanency of the Return that it might be well to examine. It is called The Great week of Human History, and is based on the "Seven Days" of the "Creative week," and the declaration of Scripture (2 Pet. 3:8), "That one day is with the Lord as a Thousand Years, and a Thousand Years as one day."

The Battle of the Culture

The Millennium in the Old Testament is described as a "Sabbath Keeping" period of rest, and is referred to as such in Heb. 4:411, where it is associated with the "Seventh Day" of the "Creative Week." Now we know that the length of the Millennium is a 1000 Year (Rev. 20:1-19), and if it corresponds with the "Seventh Day" of the "Creative Week," why should not the remaining six days be of the same length? If so, and those days correspond with the past of human history, then from the date of the "Creative Week" up to the beginning of the Millennium should be 6000 years of human history. In confirmation of this we have the fact that a careful study of the genealogical tables and history of the Old Testament seem to show that from Adam to Christ was about 4000 years, or four days a thousand years each, corresponding to the first days of the "Creative Week," and from Christ down to the present time we have over 1900 years, or nearly 2 days of 1000 years each, thus making nearly 6 days of 1000 years each of human history, and as Christ is to come back before the Millennium, and all signs point to His Speedy return, then the 'theory" that the "Seven Days" of the "Creative Week" are typical of Seven "One Thousand Year Periods" is not unwarranted in Scripture. If our inference is correct, then it follows that the Return of the Lord will take place before the close of the present century, How much before is uncertain, if the Millennium is to be ushered in A.D. 2000, then the Rapture must take place at least 7 years before that. But right here we must sound a note of caution, there is too much confusion in Biblical Chronology to fix any dates with certainty, doubtless God has ordered it so, so as to keep us in doubt as to the exact date of the Lord's return. It may have been 4075 years, instead of 4004 (as generally given), from Adam to Christ, in that case we are living in the year 5993 from the creation of Adam, or on the eve of the Rapture. Again we must not forget that God uses in "Prophetical Chronology" the Calendar Year of 360 days to a year, while we use the Julian or Astronomical Years of 365 1/4 days, and it would be necessary for us to find out what kind of year is used and reduce it to the Calendar year.

Thus we might find that we are nearer the end of the six thousandth year than we aware, and that the Return of the Lord is Imminent, however, while we may look upon the above theory as suggestive and in a way confirmatory of the near coming of the Lord, it is not conclusive, and we are not warranted in fixing any date based upon it. And further, we must not forget that the Rapture may take place sometime before the "Tribulation Period" begins and Antichrist is revealed. So if we could fix the exact date when this century will close, and count back 7 years, the Rapture might occur 5,10 or even 25 years before that, so as to give time for the rebuilding of Babylon and other events that are to occur before the Tribulation Period can begin, otherwise the Rapture would not be a surprise. It is not for the Christian to look for "Times" and "Seasons" and "Signs," to do so will put him in the class of those who say: "May Lord delayed His Coming" (Luke 12:42-48), and he will become preoccupied with other things and neglect to be watchful. Let us live as if we expected the Return of our Lord at any moment. **A Practical Doctrine,** but why, you ask, should we put so much emphasis on the "Second Coming" of Christ'? Why not talk and preach about the practical affairs of life? About the social and commercial problems of the world and their solution through the Gospel? The answer is that the only way to solve these problems is for Christ to return, and the longer His "Return" is delayed, the longer it will be before these problems are solved. **1. As To The Jews,** the Jews are a downtrodden people, their only hope is the Return of the Lord, when He comes back they shall be restored to their own land and become a nation again. "Therefore, behold, the days come said the Lord, that it shall no more be said, The Lord lived, that brought up the Children of Israel out of the Land of Egypt; but the Lord lived that brought up the Children of Israel from the land of the North (Russia) and from All the Lands whither He had driven them; and I will bring them again into their land that I gave unto their father." Jer. 16:14-15; Isa. 43:5-7. And they shall never again be dispersed. "For I will set mine eyes upon them for good, and I will bring them again to this land;

and I will build them and I will bring them again to this land; and I will build them, and not pull them down; and I will plant them, and not pluck them up." Jer. 24:6, this has never as yet been fulfilled. **2. As T Jerusalem and Palestine,** "thus said the Lord Jehovah; in the day that I will cleanse you from all your iniquities I will cause the cities (of Palestine) to be inhabited, and the waste places shall be rebuilt, and the land that was desolate shall be tilled……..and the shall say, this land that was desolate is become like the garden of Eden." Ez. 36:33-35. Joel 3:18. Joel 2:24-26, "thus said the Lord of Hosts; there shall yet old men and old women dwell in the streets of Jerusalem, and every man with his staff in his hand for very age, and the streets of the city shall be full of boys and girls playing in the streets thereof." Zech. 8:4-5. Zech. 14:20-21. **3. As To the Nations.,** when the Lord Jesus Christ returns He will sit upon the "Throne of His Glory" at Jerusalem, and shall separate the "Sheep Nations" from the "Goat Nations," and only the "Sheep Nations" will survive as nations and be permitted to become part of the Millennial Kingdom. Matt. 25:31-40. these nations will become righteous, "And it shall come to pass that every one that is left of all the nations which come against Jerusalem shall even go up from year to year to worship the King, the Lord of Hosts, and to keep the "Feast of Tabernacles." Zech. 14:16. As the result of all this the nations shall beat their swords into plowshares and their spears into pruning hooks; nations shall not lift up a sword against nation, neither shall they learn war any more, But they shall sit every man under his vine and under his fig tree; and none shall make them afraid," Micah 4:3-4. Isa. 2:4. The only way then to stop wars and labor troubles and all socialistic and anarchical movements is for Christ to return and set up His Millennial Kingdom. **4. As To Satan.,** the only way to get rid of Satan and all his evil influences and power is for Christ to come back, for when He comes back Satan will be bound and cast into Bottomless Pit for 1000 years. Rev. 20:1-3. **5. As To The Earth.** Since the Fall of Man the earth has been cursed with thorns and thistles and all kinds of insect pests and disease germs, and man by the sweat of his face has been compelled to earn his daily bread.

QUESTIONING GOD

Even the brute creation became carnivorous and learned to prey upon each other, and the whole creation groaned and travailed in pain together until now." Rom. 8:22, but all this will be changed when Christ comes back, for then "the wilderness and the solitary place shall be glad for them; and the desert shall rejoice and blossom as the rose." Isa. 35:1. "Then shall the earth yield her increase," Psa. 67:6. And the ploughman will overtake the reaper, and the treaded of grapes him that "sowed seed." Amos 9:13. **The Blessed Hope,** the Second Coming of Christ is "The Blessed Hope," writing to Titus Paul said— "Looking for that Blessed Hope, and the Glorious Appearing of the Great God and Savior Jesus Christ. Titus 2:13. Most Christians when speaking of their "Hope" mean their Hope of Salvation, but we cannot hope for a thing we have and salvation is a present possession if we are trusting in Christ as our Savior, the Christian's "Hope," then is the Return of His Lord," Man is a three-fold being, he has a body, a soul, and a spirit; for him to die is to lose his body. Now he knows that he cannot get his body back until the resurrection and he also knows that there can be no Resurrection until Christ comes back. Therefore to him Christ's return is "The Blessed Hope," not only that if he dies he will then be raised, but it is to him the "Hope" that Christ will come back before he dies and he shall be "caught up" to meet Him in the air without dying. 1 Thess. 4:13-18. "The Blessed Hope" is also a "Purifying Hope," "And every man that hath this hope in him Purified Himself," I John 3:1-3. That is, everyone who is looking for the Lord's return will try to keep himself pure. It will make us "Watchful." "Watch ye therefore, for ye know not when the Master of the house cometh, at even, or at midnight, or at the cock-crowing, or in the morning; lest coming suddenly he find you sleeping. And what I say unto you I say unto all— "Watch. " Mark 13:35-37. If we are watching for the Lord we will be careful of our conduct, we will not want Him to come and find us doing questionable things, or in questionable places. We will want to hoard money, nor spend our money in an extravagant manner; we will want to lay up for ourselves treasures in heaven by contributing to missions.

The Battle of the Culture

We will see to it that in our homes there is no kind of literature, or art, or pictures, or anything that we would not like His pure eyes to see if He were to be a visitor in a home. In short, "The Blessed Hope" helps us to cling lightly to this world; it will not make us idle and negligent, but will fill us with zeal to be found faithful servants at His return. For this reason it is a noteworthy fact and a witness to the power of the doctrine, that those who believe it are the most consecrated, unselfish, and strenuous workers in the Master's service. This "Hope" will also keep us from being Ashamed at His Coming, And now, little children, abide in Him; that when He shall appear, we may have confidence, and not be ashamed before Him at His Coming." 1 John 2:28. If we are watching for Him and our house is in order, and we are ready to give a faithful account of our Stewardship we shall not be ashamed before Him at His coming. Matt. 25:14-30. The Hope of the Lord's Pre-Millennial Return fills the heart of those who believe it with joy, In Luke 24:52 we read that when Jesus was parted from His Disciples and ascended into Heaven, "they returned to Jerusalem with great joy, and were continually in the Temple, praising and blessing God." That seems strange conduct on their part, for naturally we would suppose that His Departure would have filled them with sadness, but when we recall that, when He ascended, two men stood by in white apparel and told them that Jesus would come back again, we can understand their joyfulness. Acts.1:11. It has often been said in opposition to the doctrine of the Second Coming, "If Christian people believe that Jesus is soon coming back why do they build houses and churches and make investments and plan for the education of their children and so on?' The answer is that Jesus coming back will not do away with the end for houses and churches and education. The world moved on just as before after His First Coming, and it will do the same after His Second Coming, people will need homes and churches, business will go on as before, and the unconverted children of Christian believers will be left behind and need homes and education and means to live on. The prosperity of the world will be greater during the Millennium than ever before, so there is no occasion for those who are looking for the Lord's Return to neglect the affairs of this life. What we as Christians hope for is that the Lord will come back and take us out of the world before the awful days of the "Tribulation Period" come, and then when they are over and Jesus comes back to reign we shall come back with Him as glorified beings to rule and reign over the Millennial earth, and probably visit churches where once we worshipped, and institutions that our money built. The preacher of the Doctrine of the Pre-Millennial Coming of Christ wields a "two-edged sword," the unbeliever when urged to become a Christian may say I am young and there is plenty of time and so may put off the time of decision, but when he is told that it is not a question of time, or the mere salvation of his soul, but that Jesus may be back at any time and it is a question of being ready to meet Him, then he sees the importance of immediate decision.

CHAPTER VI
WAR
IS
DECLARED

The Tribulation, the Scriptures speak of a "Great Tribulation" that is coming on the earth, Jesus in His" Olivet Discourse" uttered on the Mt. of Olives on the Tuesday evening before His Crucifixion, said— " Then shall be great tribulation, such as was not since the beginning of the world to this time, no ,nor ever shall be. And except those days should be shortened, there should no flesh be saved; but for the Elect's Sake (the elect of Israel) those days shall be shortened." Matt. 24:21, 22. That this Tribulation was not the terrible sufferings that befell the Jewish people at the time of the destruction of Jerusalem in A.D. 70, is clear, because many of the things that are happen before and after "The Great Tribulation," did not at the destruction of Jerusalem. The Fact of the Tribulation, our Lord's prophecy does not stand alone; it is backed up by other prophecies both in the Old and New Testament. Turning to the Old Testament we find in Jer. 30:4-7, that it is the time of "Jacob's Trouble," and is compared in its sufferings to the "birth-pangs" of a woman, in Ezek. 20:34-38 it is spoken of as the time when Israel shall "Pass under the Rod;" and in Ezek. 22:19-22,

The Battle of the Culture

we read how that God is going to cast Israel into His "Melting Pot," where they are to be refined as "gold is refined." Malachi 3:1-3, and Zech. 13:9. Daniel speaks of it as a "Time of Trouble" for his people, the Jews, Dan. 12:1, from these references we see that "The Great Tribulation" is something that has to do with the Jewish people, and is a Judgment through which they must pass as a "refining process" to fit them to again be God's chosen people. Indirectly the Gentiles will be affected by it, but the Church will be "caught out" before that "Great and Terrible Day of the Lord." In the New Testament we have two descriptions of it, the first is by Jesus in His Olivet Discourse, Matt.24:9-22, and the second is in the Book of Revelation, chapters 6:1 to 19:21, where in the breaking of the "Seals," the sounding of the "Trumpets" and the pouring out of the "Vials" John sees in vision the things that are to occurs during the Tribulation Period. **The "Time" of the Tribulation,** the Old Testament prophets speak of it as "That Day," and the "Latter Days," and the Prophet Joel calls it the "Day of the Lord." Joel 1:15; 2:1; 3:14. The Scriptures speak of "Four Days." 1. Man's Day that is the present Dispensation in which we are living. 2. The Day of Christ That is the day when the Lord Jesus will come and take his Church out of the world, and includes the time between the "Rapture" and the "Revelation." On earth it is the "Day of the Antichrist." 3. "The Day of the Lord," that is the day of "Vengeance of Our Lord," and includes the period of the "Great Tribulation" and the Millennium that follows. 4. That Day of God that is the period that begins with the "Renovation of the Earth by Fire" and extends to eternity. The time of the Tribulation then is "after" the Church has been "caught out," and during the reign of the Antichrist on the earth. The Prophet Daniel in His Vision of the "Seventy Weeks" (Dan. 9:20-27) was told that it would be 69 weeks from the going forth of the Edict "to restore and rebuild Jerusalem to the Messiah the Prince." Those were "Prophetic Weeks," in which each week stood for "seven" years, and they were literally fulfilled, for it was exactly 483 years of 360 days, from the going forth of that Edict, B. C. 445, until Jesus rode in triumph into Jerusalem, A.D. 30 and was hailed as the promised Son of David.

War is Declared

Dan. 9:24, the seventy weeks determines the Jews and the holy city end times of their sins humanly and nationally. It sets the time of the first coming of Christ and gives length of the reign of the Antichrist. The time that has come and gone and the time that is yet to come. The period into seventy weeks is divided into three periods, Seven Weeks...Three Score...and two Weeks and one Week.

The weeks of Scripture:

Week of Days Gen: 1-2; 3

Week of Weeks—Lev.23:9-14...Feast of First fruits...Feast of Pentecost

Week of Months---Lev. 2:1-44...Passover feast...Feast of Tabernacles

Week of Years—Ex.21:2; Lev.25:1-7 Sabbatical Years

Week of Weeks of Years---Lev. 25:6-17...Year of Jubilee

Week of Millenniums...The Original Earth to The New Earth

Week of Ages...Alpha and Omega Eph. 2:7

Within a week the Jews had Jesus crucified and then "God's Clock" stopped, and the remaining "one week, the "Seventieth," has still to be fulfilled. In the meantime, in the break between the "sixty-ninth" and "seventieth" week, the Holy Spirit is gathering out the Church, and when it is complete it will be taken away, and then "God's Clock" will begin to tick again, because He will again be dealing with His People the Jews. It is during this last, or "Seventieth Week" of Daniel's "Seventy Weeks," that the Tribulation is to occur, and as the "weeks" of the fulfilled "sixty-nine" weeks, were each "seven years" in length so this last, or "Seventieth Week," must be the same.

The length then of the "Tribulation Period" should be "seven years," but Jesus tells us in Matt. 24:22, that for the **"ELECT'S SAKE"** Those Days Shall Be Shortened. Not the "Elect" of the Church, for they are "caught out" before Tribulation, but the "Elect" of Israel, the 144,000 "Sealed Ones" of Rev. 7:1-8.

The "CHARACTER" of the Tribulation, while the "Tribulation Period" shall last for about seven years as to its severity it will be divided into two parts of three and a half years each. The second or last part so far exceeding in its severity the first part as to be known as **"The GREAT TRIBULATION."** What was to happen during Daniel's "Seventieth Week" was not revealed to Daniel. He received a communication which he did not understand and was told to "seal the Book up until the Time of the End." Dan.4, 8, 9. All Daniel knew was that the contents of the Book had reference to the "Time of Trouble" that should befall his People at the "Time of the End" (of their sorrows), not the "End of Time." What that "Sealed Book" contained is no longer a Mystery, for the Apostle John saw the "seals" of that Book broken, and was told to record what it contained. The Seven-Sealed Book of the Book of Revelation is the Book that Daniel was told to seal up. If we want to know then about what is to happen during the Tribulation, all we have to do is to read and study the Book of Revelation from Rev. 6:1 to 19:21. As the Dragon is cast out of the Heavenlies in chapter 12, and he is cast out in the "Middle of the Week," it follows that chapter's 6 to 11 inclusive cover the "First Half" of the week, or 3 1/2 years, and chapters 13 to 19 inclusive the "Second Half." Let us study each half of the Week by itself, First Half of the Week; the "Week" begins with the breaking of the "Seals." **First Seal Rev, 6:1, 2.** A "White Horse" appears, the Rider of which is uncrowned at first but is afterward crowned, and He has a bow in his hand, and goes forth conquering. This rider is not Christ, Christ as the Lamb is holding and breaking the "seals" of the Book, He does not appear as a White Horse Rider until chapter 19. The "Rider" is Antichrist, and pictures him before he is crowned and becomes the Chief Ruler of the "Ten Federated Kingdoms" of the revived Roman Empire.

War is Declared

He is the "Prince who is to come," and who shall "confirm the Covenant" with the Jews for "one week." Dan. 9:26, 27. This proves that Antichrist appears at the "beginning" of the "Week" and not in the "Middle" as some claim. **Second Seal, Rev. 6:3, 4.** A "Red Horse" appears, the Rider of which has power to take peace from the earth. The symbolism is clear, Red, the color of the horse, is a symbol of "blood," and the **"SWORD OF WAR"** the time is clearly that prophesied by Christ. Matt. 24:6, 7. The outcome of these wars will probably be the "Ten Kingdom Federation" over which Antichrist shall become the head. **Third Seal, Rev. 6:5, 6.** A "Black Horse" appears, the Rider of which holds a pair of scales in his hand a voice cries—" A measure of wheat for a penny, and three measures of barley for a penny; and do not damage the oil and wine." The meaning is clear, when all able-bodied men are drafted for **"WAR"** the fields remain untilled and famine follows, just as Christ prophesied. Matt. 24:7. The olive and the grape do not need cultivation, so their ruthless destruction is forbidden. **Fourth Seal, Rev. 6:7, 8.** A "Pale Horse" appear, the Rider of which is "Death," it is noteworthy that the Riders of the first three horses are not named. They will be recognized when they appear. Hell (Hades) follows in the wake of "Death" ready to swallow up his victims caused by war and famine. **Fifth Seal, Rev. 6:9-11.,** When the Fifth Seal was broken John saw the "souls of martyrs" (**The Nation**) under the Altars. These Martyrs, whose "souls" John saw are not the Martyrs of the "past ages;" they were taken up with the Church but the Martyrs who will be killed for the "Word of their Testimony, and who love not their lives to the death" (Rev.12; 11), during the Tribulation. After the Church is caught out the preaching of the "Gospel of the Kingdom" will be restored. Matt. 24:14. as it is a proclamation that Christ is about to set up an "Earthly Kingdom," it will be exceedingly distasteful to Antichrist and his followers, and a "Great Persecution" will follow. Matt. 9-13. It is the "souls" of the martyrs of the Persecution that John saw under the Altar, they asked that their death should be avenged, but were told to rest for a "little season" until they were joined by their fellow servants and brethren who should die as they did. The promise is fulfilled in Rev. 20:4, **Sixth Seal. Rev.6:12-17.**

The Battle of the Culture

When the Sixth Seal is broken great "physical changes" will occur on the earth. Joel 2:30, 31; Matt. 24:29; Isa 13: 9-11. So terrible will these changes be that men will call upon the mountains and rocks to fall and hide them from the wrath of the Lamb, the 24th chapter of Matthew should be compared with Rev. 6:1-17. Between the breaking of the "Sixth" and "Seventh" Seals there will be a pause or interval, during which 144,000 of Children of Israel, 12,000 from each of the Twelve Tribes, will be sealed. As there were 7000 in Ahab's time who would not bow the knee to Baal (1 Kings 19:18), so in the Tribulation there shall be 144,000 of Antichrist. They are "sealed" by an angel, and the "Seal" is imprint of the "Father's Name" on their foreheads. Rev.14:1; 22:4. Then John saw a **"Blood Washed Multitude." Rev.7:9-17.** This introduces us to another class of saved of the "End Time," they are not the Church, for they come out of the "Great Tribulation." They are the Nations who accept Christ as their Savior after the Church is caught out. They are saved and shall serve God in His Heaven temple, and never hunger or thirst any more, but they are not part of the Church and shall not participate in any millennial blessings on earth. **Seventh Seal, Rev.8:1.** At the breaking of the "Seventh Seal" there will be "silence in Heaven" for a limited period. This will be a period of preparation for the greater conflict to follow, following the "Silence," Seven Angels in succession sound upon Seven Trumpets. **First Trumpet, Rev. 8:7,** When the "First Trumpet" sounds "hail" and "fire mingled with blood" will be cast upon the earth and a "third part of the trees" and "all green grass" will be "burnt up." This will be a fulfillment of Joel 2:30, 31. This is a repetition of the "Seventh Egyptian Plaque." Ex. 9:22-26 That was "literal," Why should this not be? **Second Trumpet, Rev. 8:8, 9,** When the "Second Trumpet" sounds a "burning mountain," probably a Meteor, will fall into the sea (Mediterranean) and will destroy a "third part of the creatures of the sea " and a "third part of the ships," probably some fleets assembled for a naval battle, and the "blood" of the destroyed will discolor a third part of the sea. **Third Trumpet, Rev. 8:10, 11.**

War is Declared

When the "Third Trumpet" sounds a "great burning star," called "Wormwood," will fall from the heavens and poison the streams of fresh water. This will probably be another Meteor that in exploding will fill the atmosphere with "noxious gases," that will be absorbed by the rivers and fountains of water, and poison them, so as to cause the death of all who drink of them. Wormwood is used in the manufacture of "Absinthe," an intoxicating beverage much used France, and poisonous, the Prophet Jeremiah refers to this time. Jer. 9:13-15. **Fourth Trumpet, Rev. 9:1-12 "First Woe," "The Plaque of Locusts."** When the "Fifth Trumpet" sounds a "Star" will fall from heaven to the earth with the "key" of the **"Bottomless Pit."** This is not a real star, but an Angel who will look like a Star, for to him was given the Key. He will not be a "Fallen Angel or Satan himself as some suppose, for God would not entrust the Key of the "Bottomless Pit" to Satan, but he will be the "same Angel" that will bind Satan and cast him into the "Bottomless Pit" for 1000 year. Rev.20:1-3. When the "Bottomless Pit" is opened, a cloud like smoke of "locust" will emerge and cover the earth, they will be a combination of horse, man, woman, lion and scorpion. The "sound of their wings" will be as the sound of chariots of many horses running to battle. Their size is not given, but they will doubtless be much larger than ordinary locusts, but they will not be them, for ordinary locusts feed on vegetation, but these locusts will be forbidden to hurt the grass or the trees, or any green thing, and only be permitted to afflict "men," and only those they shall not be permitted to "kill," but only "torment." The meaning of this scourge of "Scorpion Locusts" seems to be that a vast army of "Demons" will be liberated from the "Bottomless Pit," who shall enter into and take possession of the "bodies" of men, and so "torment" them that they shall desire to die and shall not be able, the demons preventing them. The "Scorpion Locusts" have a king, which ordinary locusts have not. Prov. 30:27. This king's name in the Hebrew is "Abaddon," but in the Greek is "Apollyon." The word means "destroyer," this king is not Satan, Satan is at liberty, while the king of the Bottomless Pit" is confined with his subjects.

Sixth Trumpet, Rev. 9:13-21. "Second Woe," "The Plaque of Horseman." When the "Sixth Trumpet" shall sound a voice from the "Golden Altar" will command the Trumpeter to loose "four angels" which are bound in the great river Euphrates. That they are "Bad Angels" is seen from the fact that they are "bound" and they are the leaders of an army of 200,000,000 "Infernal Calvary." This Calvary will not be composed of ordinary men and horses. The horses will have the "body" of a Horse, the "head" of a Lion, a "Tail" like a serpent, with the "head of a serpent" at its end. Out of their mouths will issue "fire," "smoke" and "brimstone," and by these three the "third part of men will be killed and the sting of their "serpent tails" will cause great pain. The riders upon these horses will have "breastplates of fire and brimstone" to match the breath of the horses. Supernatural armies are not unknown to Scriptures. 2 Kings 6: 13-17. When Jesus returns He will be accompanied by the Armies of Heaven, and it stands to reason that Satan has his armies. Awful as this "demon" invasion will be it will not cause men to repent. According to the Revised Versions verse 15 should read: "The four angels were loosed which had been prepared for the Hour and Day and Month and Year." That is, the Four Angels now bound in the Euphrates will be loosed in the Exact Year, Month, Day and even Hour predetermined by God for the "Demon Invasion," and not, as some think, to slay for a year, month and day, or 391 days. These two invasions of "Scorpion Locusts and Infernal Calvary" warn us that in the days after the Church is caught out, Satan and his "Demon Forces" will be increasingly active and do all they can to torment and destroy mankind. **The Interval,** Between the sounding of the "Sixth" and "Seventh Trumpets" there will be an "Interval," just as there was between the breaking of the "Sixth" and "Seventh Seals." During this "Interval" a "Mighty Angel" will come down from Heaven having a "Little Book" (open) in his hand. This Mighty Angel will be Christ Himself, for the description of Him corresponds with chapter 1:12-15, and as His voice is like that of a Lion, this identifies Him as the "Lion of the Tribe of Judah" of chapter 5:5; and in chapter 11:3,

War is Declared

He speaks of the "Two Witnesses" as "My Witnesses," When the "Mighty Angels" shall set His Right Foot on the sea and His "Left Foot" on the earth and lift up His Hand to Heaven, and speak that there shall be "Time no Longer" He shall take formal possession of the Earth. The expression, "Time no Longer" should read, as in the Revised Versions (margin), "No longer Delay," for Time does not end until the close of the "Perfect Age." While Christ at this time will take formal possession of the earth, actual possession will be secured until He comes again to the Mt. of Olives, at the close of the Tribulation. **The Two Witnesses,** In chapter 11: 1-14 we are given a description of "Two Witnesses" who are to prophesy during the greater part of the last half of the Week. Who they will be is very clear, one has "power to shut heaven that it rain not in the days of their prophecy." This can be no other than Elijah who was translated that he might come again before the "Great and Terrible Day of the Lord" (Malachi 4: 5,6), and who will shut up the heavens for 42 months, 3 1/2 years, which is exactly the length of time he did it in the days of Arab. The other Witness will have power over waters to turn them to blood, and to smite the earth with all plagues as often as he will. This identifies him as Moses, for he is the only person mentioned in the Scriptures who had such power, and it was for his purpose that he raised from the dead. Jude 9. As Moses and Elijah appeared together on the Mount of Transfiguration with Christ and as they probably were the two men in white apparel (angel-like) that testified at the Ascension to Christ's coming again (Acts 1:10, 11), what more probable than that they are the "Two Witnesses" who will return to the earth to announce that Coming? During their witnessing they will have power to destroy their enemies with "fire" that shall issue from their months, but at end of 1260 days they will be slain and their bodies lay exposed in the streets of the city of Jerusalem for 3 1/2 days, when they shall rise and ascend to Heaven to the amazement of those who see them go. Their ascent will be followed by a destructive earthquake, which completes the "Second Woe," **Seventh Trumpet. Rev. 11:15-19, Third Woe,"**

The Battle of the Culture

The "Seventh Trumpet" includes all that follows down to the end of chapter nineteen, one must not forget in   studying of the Book of Revelation that the "Seventh Seal" includes the "Seven Trumpets and the "Seven Vials," and that the "Seventh Trumpet" includes the "Seven Vials," for the "Seventh Seal," and the "Seventh Trumpets," and the "Seventh Vial" all end alike with voices thundering, lightning and earthquake. Rev.8; 5, 11:19; 16:18, **Middle of the Week, Rev. 12:1-17,** in the "Middle of the Week" two "Wonders" shall appear in Heaven. The Revised Versions calls them "signs," "that are they are "symbols" of something. The first will be a "Sun-Clothed Woman," this Woman is neither the Virgin Mary, nor the Church, she is Israel. We have only to be reminded of Joseph's Dream of the "sun" and "moon" and the eleven stars (Gen. 37:9), to see that this   "Sun-Clothed Woman, with the moon under her feet and upon her head a crown of "Twelve Stars," is Jewish in character. Joseph was the twelfth star. Israel is again and again compared to a "married" woman in the Old Testament, but the Church is a "Virgin," and only an espoused virgin at that. 2 Cor. 11:2. This "Woman" is   described as being with child and traveling to be delivered, when was the Church in such condition? Paul says of Israel, "Of whom as concerning the flesh Christ Came," Rom. 9: 4, 5. And Israel looked forward to the time when she could say— unto us a Child is born, unto us a Son is given." Isa. 9:6, 7. But before that could happen, Israel had to pass through many sore affliction and judgments. These were her "Travail Time" as the result of her travail the Women brought forth a "Man Child" who was to rule the nations with a "Rod of Lion, " there can be no question as to who is meant by the "Man Child." The 2 Psalm settles that, He is the Chris, who at His   Ascension was caught up and seated on His Father's Throne. After her child is delivered the Woman "flees into the Wilderness" where she hath place prepared of God, and where she is fed for 1260 days. Here is where many interpreters make a mistake, they overlook the fact that between the "fifth" and "sixth" verses of this chapter (Rev. 12 ;) the present "Church Period" comes in.

War is Declared

Here is the "gap" between the "Sixty-ninth" and Seventieth" Weeks of Daniel's "Seventy Weeks," John jumps over this "gap," from the Ascension of Christ to the casting out of Satan, because he is not dealing in these Tribulation chapters with the Church but with Israel, and wishes to continue her history without a break. Here is further evidence that the "Woman" is not the Virgin Mary, for she does not flee in Egypt, but into the Wilderness, neither does she flee with her child, for that was caught up to the Throne of God; neither does she flee for her child's "protection," but for her own **The Dragon.** The Second "Wonder" that will appear in Heaven will be a **"Great Red Dragon,"** We are not left in doubt as to who is meant, for in verse 9 he is called that "Old Serpent," "The Devil," and "Satan," His color is red the color of blood for he was a murderer from the beginning. John 8:44. The "Stars of Heaven" attached to his "tail" reveal the fact that Satan will lead astray a third of the Angels, for the Angels are spoken of as "Stars" in the Old Testament. Job, 38:7. They will be cast to the earth with him, the casting out of the Dragon is described in verse 7 to 12, His expulsion will start a War in Heaven that the Dragon has not yet been cast out Heaven is clear. He had access to God in the days of Job, 2000 years before Christ Job 1:1-2:8, He tried to destroy the "Man-Child" (Christ) at the hand of Herod when He was born. Matt. 2:16-18. He was at liberty to tempt Christ in the Wilderness, and to sift Peter, He is today the "Prince of the Powers of the Air," Eph. 2:2, and the "God of this World" (age). 2 Cor. 4:14, when the "Dragon" is cast out of the Heavenlies there will be great rejoicing in Heaven because the "Accuser" of Christ's "Brethren" (the Jews) is cast down, but there will be "woe" for the "inhabitants of the earth," for the "Dragon" will be filled with "great wrath" because he knows that he will have but a "short time" (3 1/2 yrs) to vent his wrath on the inhabitants of the earth before he is chained and cast into the bottomless Pit. When the "Dragon" is cast out, knowing that his defeat has been brought about by the elevation of the "Man-Child" to the place of power he will concentrate his hatred and malice on the "Woman" (Israel) who gave Him birth.

The Battle of the Culture

To the "Woman" will be given the "wing" of a great eagle," that she may fly into the "Wilderness," into her place where she shall be nourished for a "Time, Times, and Half a Time," or 3 1/2 years. This takes us back to the flight of Israel from Egypt, of which God said— "You yourselves have seen what I did to the Egyptians, and how I bore you on eagles wings and brought you to myself. Ex. 19:4. As the "Woman" and the "Dragon" are symbols so are the "Eagle's Wings," they speak of the rapid and safe flight of the "Woman" (Israel) into the "Wilderness," where she shall be safely kept and nourished for 3 1/2 years until the "Dragon" is bound. **The Cities of Refuge,** The "Cities of Refuge" of Old Testament times are a type of this "Wilderness Refuge" of the Children of Israel. The "Cities of Refuge" were designated cities, 3 on each side the river Jordan, where the "Man-Slayer" could flee for safety from the "Avenger of Blood." If it was proved after trial that he had slain a man "willfully," he was turned over to the "Avenger of Blood," but if he did it unwittingly, his life was spared, but he had to remain in the city until the death of the High Priest. If there were no "Man-Slayer" there would be no "Avenger of Blood," and therefore no need for a City of Refuge. Now if I find in the New Testament that a certain class of people are called upon to flee to a Place of Refuge for the protection of their lives, then I must believe that they flee because an "Avenger" of Blood" is after them, and that they flee because they are guilty of "Manslaughter." Such a class of people I find in the Jewish Race. They were the cause of the death of Christ, and though He was crucified by the Roman authorities they assumed the guilt for cried— "His blood be on Us and on Our Children." Matt. 27:25. At first it looks like willful murder, yet from the prayer of Jesus on the Cross— "Father, forgive them for they know not what they do," it is clear that Jesus death was not so much a premeditated murder as it was a murder committed in a blind religious frenzy. Paul says— "Had they known they would have crucified the "Lord of Glory." 1 Cor. 2:8. It is clear then that the Jewish race is only guilty of "Manslaughter" As the "Man-Slayer" of Jesus they have been for over 1800 years running for a "City of Refuge" and have not as yet reached it.

War is Declared

The "Avenger of Blood" has been on their track and has hounded them from nation to nation, and the epithet of The **Wandering Jew** has followed them down the centuries, and the prophecy of Moses is being fulfilled that they should find no rest for the sole of their foot. Deut. 28:64-67. If the Jews are the "Man-Slayer" who is the "Avenger of Blood? Antichrist, if the "Avenger of Blood" must be a "Kinsman" of the main slain, that means that he must be of the same "Race," and the nearest kinsman alive at the time vengeance is sought. While Jesus was the "first born" of the Virgin Mary, he was not the only child she had, she afterwards had by Joseph four sons, James, Joseph, Judas and Simon, and there were daughters. Two of these brothers of Jesus filled a large place in the Church in the first century, James was pastor of the church of Jerusalem, and Judas (also called Jude) wrote the Epistle of Jude. The kinsfolk of Jesus occupied a place by themselves for long time after Jesus passed away, and could be traced as late as A. D. 324. Somewhere in the world today, without doubt, are living some of the "Kinsfolk" of the Lord Jesus. They may not be able to trace their descent back to Jesus, but God knows where they are, and who they are and who dare deny that when the time comes for the manifestation of the Antichrist, that the "Avenger of Blood" shall be a Jew, who is a lineal descendant of the family of Jesus. And now as to the "City of Refuge" that God will provide for Israel when the "Avenger of Blood" (Antichrist), who shall then be indwelt by the Dragon, is on her track. In Isa. 26:20 we read — "Come, my people, enter into your rooms and close your doors behind you; Hide for a little while until indignation runs its course." Isa. 26:20. The context shows that this refers to the time when Antichrist, the "Avenger of Blood," will seek to destroy the Jewish people, and is the time referred to by Christ in Matt. 24:15-22. When the Lord God brought the Children of Israel out of Egypt they journeyed from the Red Sea, for a while at Mt. Sinai to receive the Law and build the Tabernacle, until they came, one year, after leaving Egypt, to Kadesh Barnea. There they sent up spies to spy out the land Canaan, but refused to go up and take possession of the land, and were compelled to wander in the Wilderness south of the Dead Sea.

The Battle of the Culture

There God took care of them and fed them for 40 years, now it is in the same Wilderness that God to provide for them a place of "Refuge" in the day when the "Avenger of Blood" shall seek to destroy them. Speaking of the Antichrist, the Prophet Daniel says— "He shall enter also into the Glorious Land (Palestine) and many countries shall be overthrown; but these shall escape out of the hand, even Edom and Moab and the chief of the Children of Ammon." Dan. 11:41. Now Edom takes in the Wilderness where Israel wandered for 40 years, and it is here in Edom that the "City of Refuge" that God has provided for Israel is located, and is known today as Petra, it was a great commercial center in the days of King Solomon. In A. D. 105 the Romans conquered the country and called the province Arabia Petra. When the power of Rome waned Petra gradually fell into the hands of the Arabs and became completely lost to the civilized world in the seventh century, and remained so until was rediscovered by Burckhardt in 1812. It is located in the mountains like as in the crater of a volcano, It has but one entrance, and that is through a narrow winding defile or canyon from 12 to 40 feet wide, the sides of which are precipitous and at time so close together as to almost shut out the blue sky above and make you think you think you are passing through a subterranean passage way. The height of the sides varies from 200 to 1000 feet, and the Length of the canyon is about two miles, no other city in the world has such a wonderful gateway. The sides of the canyon are lined with wonderful monuments and temples carved out the rocky sandstones of the sides. One inside the rocky enclosure of the city we find the ruins of magnificent buildings, tombs and monuments, the cliffs that surround the city are carved and honeycombed with excavations to a height of 300 feet above feet above the floor above of the valley, and the excavations cut as they are out of different colored strata of the rock, such as red, purple, blue, black, white and yellow, lend a beauty to their appearance that is indescribable and overpowering to the beholder. When the time come for the for the "Man-Slayer" (Israel), to escape from the hands of the "Avenger of Blood" (Antichrist), the rocky fastness of the ancient city of Petra will be her "City of Refuge,"

War is Declared

we read that when the "Woman" (Israel) shall flee into the Wilderness that the "Serpent" (Antichrist, indwelt by Satan) shall cast a flood of water out of his mouth after her to destroy her, but that the earth shall open her mouth and swallow the flood. That is Antichrist will send his army after the Israelites, and it will probably be swallowed up in a "Sand storm" of the desert, and Israel shall safely reach her place of refuge, where she be safe, not until the death of the High Priest, but until the return of "The High Priest" (Jesus), from Heaven, who as "King-Priest" of the Armies of Heaven will deliver her and allow her place refuge. **Last Half of the Week,** Filled with wrath at the escape of the "Sun-Clothed Woman," the Dragon will turn his plans he will give to the "Beast" (Antichrist) his "Power" and his "Seat," and "Great Authority." Rev. 13:2. While Antichrist, as Antichrist, exists from the beginning of the "Week," for at that time he makes a covenants for one week, (Dan. 9:27); in the "Middle of the Week" he will break the Covenant, and for the last half of the week his reign will be terrible, and the change in his character, and the character of his reign, can only be accounted for on the basis that the Dragon has incarnated himself in him. It is this phase of the reign of "Antichrist" that is brought out in the 13th chapter of the Book of Revelation. John tells us that he saw two Beasts, the first came up out of the sea, this represents "Antichrist" after his incarnation by the "Dragon," the second came up out of the earth and is called the "False Prophet." Suffice it to say that for balance of the 'Week," no man can buy or sell unless he has the "Brand of Hell," and "Mark of the Beast," on his Right Hand, or in his Forehead. At this time three "Angel Messengers" will be sent forth, the first will be a preacher of the Gospel. This is the first time an angels is commissioned to preach the Gospel, but it will not be the Gospel of the "Grace of God," (Acts 20:24), nor the Gospel for "The Kingdom" (Matt. 24:14), but a new Gospel, called the "Everlasting Gospel." Its burden is "Judgment" not "Salvation," and it will be "Good News" all those passing through the "fiery trial" of those day, for it will be the announcement that the "Hour of Judgment" is come for all that do wickedly.

The Battle of the Culture

The second "Angel Messenger" will announce the "Fall of Babylon." This is by way of anticipation, for the City of Babylon is not destroyed until after the pouring out of the "Vials," the third "Angels Messenger" will utter an awful warning to those who are tempted to worship the Beast. Declaring that if they do, they shall drink of the wine of the "Wrath of God," and shall be tormented with "fire" and "Brimstone" Forever and Ever. At this time preparation will be made in Heaven for the **Harvest and Vintage** of the earth. This is not the Harvest of the Church, that took place before the beginning of the "Week," This is the Harvest of the Gentile nations; it begins with the pouring out of the "Vials," and ends with the Battle of Armageddon. **First Vial, Rev.16: 1, 2.** When the "First Vial" is poured out a "noisome and grievous sore" will fall upon the men who have the "Mark of the Beast." and who "worship his Image." This is a repetition of the "Sixth Egyptian Plague." Ex. 9:8-12. If that was literal why should this not be? The "literalness" of these "Vial Judgments" is the key to the literalness of the whole Book of Revelation. **Second Vial, Rev. 16:3.** When the "Second Vial" is poured out, the sea (Mediterranean) will become as the "blood of a dead man." and every "living soul" (creature, for creatures have souls) in the die, something similar thought not so great in extent, happened when the "Second Trumpet" sounded. Rev. 8:8, 9. **Third Vial, Rev. 16:4-7.** When the "Third Vial" is poured out the "rivers" and fountain of water will become "blood." This repetition of the "First Egyptian Plague," Ex. 7:19-24. Those will be awful times when there will be nothing to quench the thirst but "blood." **Fourth Vial. Rev. 16: 8, 9.** When the Fourth Vial is poured out men will be "scorched with great heat." This is the only plague for which there is no Egyptian parallel, and as the others are literal so must it be. The Prophet Malachi refers to it, Malachi 4:1, the effect of this plague will be not to make men repent, but to cause them to blaspheme the Name of God. **Fifth Vial, Rev. 16:10, 11.** When the "Fifth Vial" is poured out there will be "darkness" over the whole Kingdom of the "Beast," and men will gnaw their tongues for pain." This will be a repetition of the Ninth Egyptian Plague."

War is Declared

Ex. 10:21-23, notice that this Plague follows the Plague of Scorching Heat," as if God will hide the sun whose heat was so hard to bear. The effect of the "Darkness" will be to make men "gnaw their tongues" for pain and for their sores, showing that these "Vial Plagues," overlap or follow each other rapidly. **Sixth Vial, Rev. 16: 12.** When the "Sixth Vial" is poured out the river Euphrates will be dried up so the Kings of the Kings of the East (India, China, and Japan) and their armies may cross over and gather for the great Battle of Armageddon. This will be a repetition of the opening of the Red Sea and of the river Jordan, the Prophet Isaiah foretells this— "Lord shall utterly destroy the tongue of the Egyptian (Red) Sea, and shake His hand over the River Dry-Shod," Isa. 11:1, 16. These nations will be gathered by "Three Unclean Spirit" like frogs, that shall come out of the mouth of the "Dragon," and the "Beast," and the "False Prophet," Rev. 16:13-16. They will be the "Spirit of Demons." the "Seducing Spirits" of those days, 1 Tim. 4:1. It was such a "Lying Spirit" that deceived King Ahab and led him to his death. 1 Kings 22: 20-38. **Seventh Vial. Rev. 16:17, 21.** When the "Seventh Vial" is poured out a "great voice," probably the voice of the One who cried on the Cross—"It is Finished," will cry—"It is Done," and there will be a "Great Earthquake" that will divide into three parts the "Great City" and the cities of the Nations (the 10 Federated Nations), London, Rome, Paris, etc and the "Great Babylon" that shall be rebuilt by that time, and whose destruction by an earthquake is foretold in chapter eighteen, will fall. This earthquake is foretold by the Prophets Zechariah, Zech. 14:4, 5. In the "Great Hail," every stone of which shall weigh a 100 pounds that will fall on men, we have a repetition of the "Seventh Egyptian Plague." Ex. 9:13-35. Hail has been one of God's engines of war He used it to discomfort the enemies of Israel at Beth-horon in the days of Joshua, Joshua 10:11. The Law required that the "blasphemer" should be "stoned" (Lev. 24:16), and the "Blasphemers" of the "End Times" shall be stoned from HEAVEN.

The Battle of the Culture

In the Book of Revelation, between the pouring out of the Vials and the "Battle of Armageddon," which ends the "Tribulation Period," in chapter seventeen and eighteen, there is an account of the destruction of a "System" called "**Mystery, Babylon the Great,**" and a city called Babylon. They are mentioned not because they did not exist until that time, but because at that time they are both destroyed. **Battle of Armageddon, Rev. 19:11-21.** The "Tribulation Period "will close with the great "Battle of Armageddon." As we have seen the armies of the East and the West will be assembled in the Holy Land by the "Demon Spirits" that shall be sent forth from the mouths of the "Satanic Trinity." The field of battle will be the "Valley of Megiddo," located in the heart of Palestine, the battlefield of the great battles of Old Testament. The forces engaged will be the "Allied Armies" of Antichrist on the one side, and the "Heavenly Army" of Christ on the other. The "Time" will be when the "Harvest of the Earth" IS RIPE, (Rev. 14:15), and at the "Psychological Moment" when the "Allied Armies" of Antichrist are about to take the city of Jerusalem. The Prophet Zechariah says— "Behold a day is coming for the Lord when spoil taken from you will be divided among you. For I will gather all the nations against Jerusalem to battle, and the city will be captured, the houses plundered, the women ravished and half of the city exiled, but the rest of the people will not be cut off from the city. Then the **Lord will go forth and fight against those nations as when He fights on a day of battle.** Zech. 14:1-3. This "going forth" is graphically described I Rev. 19:11-21, when He came the first time to Jerusalem as King, He rode on a "colt," the foal of an ass, (Matt. 21:1-11), this time He shall come on a "White Horse," His eyes will be as a "flame of fire" and on His head shall be "many crowns," and He shall be clothed in a vesture "dipped in blood." Not His own blood but the blood of His enemies. The Prophet Isaiah foresaw that day—Who is this who comes from Edom, with garments of glowing colors from Bozrah, this One who is majestic in His apparel, Marching in the greatness of His strength? "It is I who speak in righteousness, mighty to save."

War is Declared

Why are your apparel red and your garments like the one who treads in the wine press? I have trodden the wine trough alone, and from the peoples there was no man with me. I also trod them in My anger And trampled them in my wrath; And their lifeblood is sprinkled on My garments, And I stained all My raiment. For the day of vengeance was in my heart, and my year of redemption has. "I looked and there was no one to help, and I was astonished and there was no one to uphold; so My own arm brought salvation to Me, I trod down the peoples in My anger and made them drunk in My wrath, And I poured out their lifeblood on the earth." Isa. 63:1-6. That this does not refer to Christ's atonement on the Cross is clear, for the Prophet adds— "For the Day of Vengeance" is in mine heart, and the year of my is come." There was no "vengeance" in Christ's heart on the Cross. It was "Father forgive them for they know not what they do," The time the Prophet foretells, is the "Day of Christ's Vengeance" on His enemies, and the day when He shall redeem His chosen people the Jews from the power of Antichrist. It is the time when He shall tread— **"The Winepress Of the Fierceness and Wrath of Almighty God."** The Apostle John had a vision of this "Winepress" in chapter fourteen verses 14 to 20. That was before the pouring out of the "Vials," and was a prophetic fore view of what should happen in chapter nineteen. In verse 18 to 20, and angel with a "sharp sickle" is told to— "Thrust in thy Sharpe Sickle, and gather the clusters of the 'Vine of Earth," and gather the clusters of the Vine of the Earth for her grapes are fully ripe. And the angel thrust in his Sickle into the earth, and gathered of the Vine of the Earth, and cast into the Great Winepress of the wrath of God." And we read that "The Winepress was trodden Without the City, and blood, (not wine), came out of the Winepress, even unto the horses bridles, by the space of a Thousand and Six Hundred Furlongs." From this we see that the 'Allied Armies" of Antichrist will cover the whole of Palestine, and so great shall be the slaughter, that, in the valleys and hollows, all over the whole of Palestine, for the length of Palestine as far south as Bozrah is 1600 furlongs or 200 miles the blood shall be up to the horses bridles. It will be the time of which Isaiah speaks, when the land shall be "Soaked with Blood." Isa. 34:1-8.

The Battle of the Culture

So great will be the carnage, God will prepare for it in advance, "And I saw an angels standing in the sun; and he cried with a loud voice, saying to all the fowls that fly in the in the midst of Heaven, (Buzzards, Vultures, Eagles, etc), Come and gather yourselves together unto the SUPPER OF THE GREAT GOD, Then I saw an angel standing in the sun, and he cried out with a loud voice, saying to all the birds which fly in mid-heaven, Come, assemble for the great supper of God, so that may eat the flesh of kings and the flesh of kings and the flesh of commanders and the flesh of mighty men and the flesh of horses and of those who sit on them and the flesh of all men, both free men and slaves, and small and great" Rev. 19:17, 18. This "Feast" described in the Old Testament. "And, the son of man, thus says the Lord God, speaks to every feathered fowl, and to every beast of the field, Assemble yourselves, and come gather yourselves on every side to My Sacrifice, that I do sacrifice upon the Mountain of Israel, that you may eat flesh and drink blood. You shall eat the flesh of the Mighty, and drink the blood of the Princes of the Earth, of rams, of lambs, of goats, of bullocks, all of them fatlings of Bashan. And you shall eat fat till you are full, and drink blood till you be drunken. . .Thus you shall be filled at My Table with horses and chariots (their occupants), with Mighty Men and with all Men of War, says the Lord God," Ez. 39:1-22. And in the same chapter we are chapter we are told that the "House of Israel," the occupants of Palestine in that day, shall seven months burying the bones of the dead, the flesh having been eaten by the birds and beasts of prey, and the wood from the weapons of warfare, army wagons, spears, etc, shall last the inhabitations of the land for fuel seven years, so that they will not have to take wood out of the field, nor cut down any of the forests. The words in Rev. 19:21, "and all the fowls were filled with their flesh," declare that those "Fowl Guests" will be **GORGED WITH CARRION.** Then will be fulfilled the words of Jesus— "For wheresoever's the carcass is, there will the Eagles (birds of prey) be gathered together." Matt. 24:27, 28. The eagle feeds mainly on fresh meat; the Hebrews classed the eagle among the birds of prey, such as the vulture.

War is Declared

The destruction of this great army will be brought about by the "sword" of Him who will head the Armies of Heaven; the "sword" that proceeds out of the mouth of the White Horse Rider is not the "Sword of the Spirit," for that brings "Salvation," not destruction. The "sword" stands for some supernatural means of destruction, and as there is to be a "Great Hail" to fall from Heaven upon the enemies of God at this time, that may be the means God will use for it was in the way that the enemies of Israel were destroyed on the same battle held in the "Battle of Beth-Horon" in the days of Joshua 10:1-11. The issue of the "Battle of Armageddon" will never be in doubt. The previous summoning of the birds and beasts of prey, prove this, Before the destruction of the army of Antichrist, he and the False Prophets will be cast "alive" into the "Lake of Fire," This shows that they are not "Systems" but "Persons," and as Enoch and Elijah were taken to Heaven without dying, so Antichrist and the False Prophet will be cast into the "Lake of Fire" without dying, and will be still there and alive when Satan is cast in a 1000 years later. Before Antichrist is seized and cast into the "Lake of Fire," Satan will make his exit from his person, and after the battle is over, Satan will be bound and cast into the "Bottomless Pit," where he will be "sealed up" for 1000 years. This is the culminating act of the "Tribulation Period.

CHAPTER VII

DEATH

AND

DESTRUCTION

BABYLON THE GREAT, Ecclesiastical Babylon Mystery, Rev. 17:1-18, that the ancient city of Babylon restored is to play an important part in the startling events of the days of this Dispensation, is very clear. This is seen from what is said of it in seventeenth and eighteenth chapters of the Book of Revelation. At first sight the two chapters, which contain some things in common. Are difficult to reconcile, but when we get the "Key" the reconciliation is easy. The seventeenth chapter speaks of a "Woman," and this "Woman" is called "Mystery," Babylon the Great, The Mother of the Harlots and Abomination of the Earth." The Eighteenth chapter speaks of a "City," a literal city, called "Babylon the Great," That the "Woman" and the "City" do not symbolize the same thing is clear, for what is said of the "Woman" do not apply to a city, and what is said of the "City" does not apply to a woman. The "Woman" is destroyed by the "Ten Kings," while the "Kings of the Earth" in the next chapter, "bewail and lament" the destruction of the "City," which is not destroyed by them, but by a mighty earthquake and fire. Again the "Woman" is destroyed Three and a Half Years Before the City; and the fact that the first of chapter eighteen says— after these things," that is after the destruction of the "Woman" what happens to the "City" occurs, shows that the "Woman" and the "City" are not the same.

The Battle of the Culture

The Woman's name is Mystery, Babylon the Great," Mystery!" Where have we heard that word before, and in what connection? Paul calls the Church a Mystery because it is not known to the Old Testament Patriarchs and Prophets. Eph. 3:1-21. That Christ was to have a "bride" was first revealed to Paul (Eph 5:23-32) and the "Mystery" that Antichrist is have a "bride" was first revealed to john on the Isle of Patmos. The name of Antichrist's "bride" is "Babylon" the Great." Someone may ask why give to a "bride" the name of a 'City"? The answer is that it is not unusual in the Scriptures. When the same angels that showed John in this chapter "Mystery, Babylon the Great," came to him in chapter 21:9-10 and said— "Come, I will show you the Bride—"The Lamb's Wife," he showed John, instead of a woman, that great City, the "Holy Jerusalem" descending out Heaven from God. Here we see that a "city" is called abide. Mystery, Babylon the Great, the bride of Antichrist, then, is not a literal city, but a "System," a religious and apostate "System." As the Church, the Bride of Christ, is composed of regenerated followers of Christ, so "Mystery, Babylon the Great," the bride of Antichrist, will be composed of the followers of all False Religions. The river Euphrates, on which the city of Babylon was built was one of the four branches into which the river that flowed through the Garden of Eden was divided, and Satan doubtless chose the site of Babylon as his headquarters from which to sally forth to tempt Adam and Eve. It was doubtless here that the Antediluvian Apostasy had its source that ended in the Flood. To this center the "forces of Evil" gravitated after the flood, and "Babel" was the result. This was the origin of the nations, but the nations were not scattered abroad over the earth until Satan had implanted in them the "Virus" of a doctrine that has been the source of the every false religion the world has ever known. Babel, or Babylon, was built by Nimrod. Gen. 10:8-10, it was the seat of the first great Apostasy, here the "Babylonian Cult" was invented, a system claiming to posses the highest wisdom and to reveal the divines secrets. Before a member could be initiated he had to "confess" to the Priest, the Priest then had him in his power.

Death and Destruction

This is the secret of the power of the Priests of the Roman Catholic Church today, once admitted into this order men were no longer Babylonians Assyrians, or Egyptians, but members of a Mystical Brotherhood, over who was placed a Pontiff or "High Priest," whose word was law. The city of Babylon continued to be the seat of Satan until the fall of the Babylonian and Medo-Persian Empires, when he shifted his Capital to Pergamos in Asia Minor, where it was in John's day. Rev. 2:12, 13. When Attalus, the Pontiff and King of Pergamos, died in B.C. 133, he bequeathed the Headship of the "Babylonian Priesthood" to Rome. When the Etruscans (Nation of Etruria) came to Italy from Lydia (the region of Pergamos), they brought with them the Babylonian religion and rites. They set up a Pontiff who was head of the Priesthood, Later the Romans accepted this Pontiff as their civil ruler. Julius Caesar made Pontiff was of the Etruscan Order in B.C. 63 he was made "Supreme Pontiff" of the "Babylonian Order," thus becoming heir to the rights and titles of the Attalus, Pontiff of Pergamos, who had made Rome his heir by will. Thus the first Roman Emperor became the Head of the "Babylonian Priesthood," and Rome the successor of Babylon, The Emperors of Rome continued to exercise the office of "Supreme Pontiff" until A. D. 376, when the Emperor Gratian, for Christian reasons, refused it. The Bishop of the Church at Rome, Damascus, was elected to the position. He had been Bishop 12 years, having been made Bishop in A. D. 366, through the influence of the monks of Mt. Carmel, a college of Babylonian religion originally found by the priest of Jezebel. So in A. D. 378 the Head of the Babylonian Order became the Ruler of the "Roman Church." Thus Satan united, Rome and Babylon In One Religious System, soon after Damascus was made "Supreme Pontiff" the "rites" of Babylon began to come to the front. The worship of the Virgin Mary was set up in A.D. 381. All the outstanding festivals of the Roman Catholic Church are of Babylonian origin. Easter is not a Christian name; it means **"Ishtar,"** one of the titles of the Babylonian Queen of Heaven, whose worship by the children of Israel was such an abomination in the sight of God. The decree for observance of Easter and Lent was given in A.D. 519.

The Battle of the Culture

The "Rosary" is of Pagan origin. There is no warrant in the word of God for the use of the "Sign of the Cross." It had its origin in the mystic "Tau" of the Chaldeans and the Egyptians; It came from the letter "T" the initial name of "Tammuz," and was used in the Babylonian Mysteries for the same magic purposes as the Romish Church now employs it. Celibacy, the Tonsure , and the Order of Monks and Nuns, have no warrants or authority from Scripture. The Nuns are nothing more than an imitation of the "Vestal Virgins" of Pagans Rome. As to the word "Mystery" the Papal Church has always shrouded herself in mystery of "Baptismal Regeneration; the mystery of "Miracle and Magic" whereby the simple memorials of the Lord's Supper are changed by the mysterious word "Transubstantiation," from simple bread and wine into the literal body and Blood of Christ; the mystery of the "Holy Water;" the Mystery of Lights on the Altar, the "Mystery Plays and other superstitious rites and ceremonies mumbled in a language that tends to Mystery and tends to confusion which is the meaning of the word Babylon. All this was a "Mystery" in John's day because the "Papal Church" had not as yet developed; though the "Mystery of Iniquity" was already at work (2 Thess. 2:7), but it is no longer a Mystery for it is now easy to identify the "Woman" —Mystery, Babylon the Great," which John described as the "Papal Church." In Rev. 17:4 we read that the "Woman" was arrayed in purple and scarlet color, and decked with gold and precious stones and pearls having a Golden Cup in her hand full of abominations and filthiness of her "fornications." Now who does not know that scarlet and purple are the colors of the Papacy? Of the different article of attire specified for the Pops to wear when he is installed into office five are scarlet. A vest covered with pearls, and a mitre, adorned with gold and precious stones was also to be worn. How completely this answers the description of the Woman's dress as she sits upon the Scarlet Colored Beast. We are also told that the Woman was "drunken with the blood of the Saints, and with the blood of the Martyrs of Jesus," While this refers more particularly to the Martyrs of the time of Antichrist, yet who does not know, who has studied the history of the of the Christian Church for the past nineteen centuries,

Death and Destruction

that this is true of the Papal Church during those centuries? One has only to read the history of the persecutions of the early Christians and more particularly the story of the "Inquisition" in Papal lands, to see that the Papal Church has been "drunk" with the blood of the Saints. The fact that the Woman sits on a " Scarlet Colored Beast" reveals the fact that at time the Beast (Antichrist) will support the Woman in her ecclesiastical pretensions, or in other words, the Woman, as a "State Church," will control and rule the State, and her long dream of world-wide Ecclesiastical Supremacy will at last be realized, for John tells us that "the waters which you saw, where the Whore sits, are Peoples, and Multitudes, and Nations and Tongues" The means that after the " True Church" (the Bride of Christ) is taken out of the world the "False" or "Papal Church" (the bride of Antichrist) will remain, and the professing body of Christians (having the form of Godliness without the power) left behind, will largely enter the Papal Church, and it will become the Universal Church. But this will continue for only a short time for the "Ten Kings" of the "Federated Kingdom," finding their power curtailed by the "Papal System" will "hate the Whore," and strip her of her gorgeous apparel, confiscate her wealth (eat her flesh) and burn her churches and cathedrals with fire. Rev. 17:16. This will occur at the time the worship of the Beast is set up, for Antichrist in his jealous hate will not permit any worship that does not center in him. The beast upon which the Woman sits is introduced to show from whom the Woman (the Papal Church) gets her power and support after the True Church has been caught out and also to show that the beast (Antichrist) and the Women (the Papal Church) are not one and the same, but separate. Therefore the Papacy is not Antichrist. From this foreview of the Papacy we see that the Papal Church is not a dying "System," that she is to be revived and become a "Universal Church," and in doing so is to commit fornication with the kings of the earth, and that she shall again that she shall again be "drunk with the blood" of the Martyrs of the Tribulation Period.

The Battle of the Culture

The meaning of chapter seventeen of the Book of Revelation is no longer a Mystery; the prophetic portrait of the Woman there given corresponds too closely with the history of the Papal Church to be a mere coincidence. **Commercial Babylon, Rev. 18:1-24, this** chapter begins with the words "after these things." What things? The things recorded in the previous chapter, the destruction of "Mystical Babylon." If "Mystical Babylon" was destroyed in the previous chapter then she cannot appear in this chapter, and the "City" here described must be a literal city called Babylon, and as there is a no city of that names on the earth today, nor has been since the ancient city of Babylon was destroyed, it must refer to some future city of Babylon. That the two chapters refer to different things is further verified by the fact that they are announced by different angels, the events of chapter seventeen are announced by one of the "Vial" Angels, while those of the eighteenth are announced by another angel; probably the "Second Angel Messenger," who by way of anticipation, announced in the chapter 14:8, "Fall of Babylon," that is there called— "That Great City." The ancient city of Babylon from the days of Nimrod (Gen. 10:10) grew in size and importance century after century until it reached its greatest glory in the reign of Nebuchadnezzar B. C. 604-562. As described by Herodotus it was an exact square of 15 miles on a side, or 60 miles around, and was surrounded by a brick wall 87 feet thick, and 350 feet high, though probably that is a mistake, 100 feet being near the height. On the wall were 250 towers, and the top of the wall was wide enough to allow 6 chariots to drive abreast, Outside this wall was a vast ditch surrounding the city, kept filled with water from the river Euphrates; and inside the wall, and not far from it, was another wall, not much inferior, but narrow, extending around the city. Twenty-five magnificent avenues, 150 feet wide, ran across the city from North to South, and the same number crossed them at right angles from East to West, making 676 great squares, each nearly three-fifths of a mile on a side, and the city was divided into two equal parts by the river Euphrates, that flowed diagonally through it, and whose banks, within the city, were walled up, and pierced with brazen gates leading down to the river.

Death and Destruction

At the ends of the main avenues, on each side of the city, were gates, whose leaves were of brass, and that shone as they were opened or closed in the rising or setting sun, like "leaves of flame." The Euphrates within the city was spanned by a bridge, at each end of which was a palace, and these palaces were connected by a subterranean passageway, or tube, underneath the bed of the river, in which at different point were located sumptuous banqueting rooms constructed entirely of brass. Near one of these palaces stood that **"Tower of Bel,"** or Babel, consisting of 8 towers, each 75 feet high, rising one upon the other, with an outside winding stairway to its summit, which towers, with the Chapel on the top, made a height of 600 feet. The Chapel contained the most expensive furniture of any place of worship in the world. On golden image alone, 45 feet high, was valued at $17,500,000, and the whole of sacred utensils were reckoned to worth $200,000,000. Babylon also contained one of the "Seven Wonders" of the world, the famous Hanging Gardens. These Gardens were 400 feet square, and were raised in terraces above the other to the height of 350 feet, and were reached by stairways 10 feet wide. The top of each terrace was covered with large stones, on which was laid a bed of rushes, then a thick layer of asphalt, next two courses of brick, cemented together, and finally plates of lead to prevent leakage; the whole was then covered with earth and planted with shrubbery and large trees. The whole had the appearance from a distance of a forest-covered mountain, which would be a remarkable sight in the level plain of the Euphrates. These Gardens were built by Nebuchadnezzar simply to please his wife, who came from the mountainous country of Media, and who was thus made contented with her surroundings. The rest of the city was, in its glory and magnificence, in keeping with these palaces, towers, and "Hanging Gardens." The character of its inhabitants and of its official life is seen in the description of "Belshazzar's Feast" in Dan. 5:1-31. Babylon was probably the most magnificent city the world has ever seen and its fall reveals what a city may become when it forsakes God and He sends His judgment upon it. It is so intimately connected with the history of God's people that the Scriptures have much to say about it.

The Battle of the Culture

A large part of the Book of Daniel and of the prophecy of Jeremiah relates to it, and it is mentioned in 11 other books of the Old Testament, and in 4 of the New Testament. And the Book of Daniel is further proven by the fact that city of Babylon is again spoken of in it, and its prominence in the affairs of the world at the "End Time" disclosed, and its final destruction foretold. That the ancient city of Babylon was destroyed there can be no question, but when we affirm that it is to be rebuilt and again destroyed we are met with two objections. 1. **That all the Old Testament prophecies in reference to its destruction have been literally fulfilled, and that it cannot be rebuilt** 2. **As there is no city of Babylon now in existence the references in the Book of Revelation to the destruction of such a city must be symbolical and not refer to a literal city.** Let us take up the first objection, for a description of Babylon and her destruction we must turn to Isaiah, chapter 13 and 14 and Jeremiah, chapter 50 and 51. In these two prophecies we find we find much that has not as yet been fulfilled in regard to the city of Babylon. The city of Babylon was captured in B. C. 541 by Cyrus, who was mentioned "by name" in prophecy 125 years before he was born. Isa 44:28-45: B.C. 712. So quietly was the city taken on the night of Belshazzar's Feast by draining the river that flowed through the city and entering by the river bed, and the gates that surmounted its banks, that the Babylonian guards had forgotten to lock that night, that some of the inhabitants did not know until the "third" day that the king had been slain and the city taken. There was no destruction of the city at that time. Some years after it revolted against Darius Hystaspis, and after a fruitless siege of nearly 20 months was taken by strategy. This was in B.C. 516, about B.C. 478 Xerxes, on his return Greece plundered and injured, if he did not destroy, the great "Temple of Bel." In B.C. 331 Alexander the Great approached the city which was then so powerful and flourishing that he made preparation for bringing all his forces into action in it should offer resistance, but the citizens threw upon the gates and received him with acclamations.

Death and Destruction

After sacrificing to Bel, he gave out that he would rebuild the vast Temple of that god, and for weeks he kept 10,000 men employed in clearing away the ruins from the foundations, doubtless intending to revive the glory of Babylon and make it his capital, when his purpose was defeated by his sudden death of marsh-fever and intemperance in his thirty-third year. During the subsequent wars of his generals Babylon suffered much and finally came under the power of Seleucus, who prompted by ambition to build a Capitol for himself, founded Seleucia in its neighborhood about B.C. 293. This rival city gradually drew off the inhabitants of Babylon, so that Strabo, who died in A. D. 25, speaks of the latter as being to a great extent deserted. Nevertheless the Jews left from Captivity still resided there in large numbers, and in A.D. 60 we find the Apostle Peter working among them, for it was from Babylon that Peter wrote his Epistle (1 Pet: 5:13), addressed "to the strangers throughout Pontus, Galatia, Cappadocia, Asia and Bithynia." About the middle of the 5th century Theodoret speaks of Babylon as being inhabited only by Jews, who had still three Jewish Universities, and in the last years of the same century the "Babylonian Talmud" was issued, and recognized as authoritative by the Jews of the whole world. In A.D. 917 Ibu Hankel mentions Babylon as an insignificant village, but still in existence. About A.D. 1100 it seems to have again grown into a town of some importance, for it was then known as the "Two Mosques." Shortly afterwards it was enlarged and fortified and received the name of Hillah, or "Rest." In A.D. 1898 Hillah contained about 10,000 inhabitants (people), and was surrounded by fertile lands, and abundant date groves stretched along the banks of the Euphrates. Certainly it has never been true that "neither shall the Arabian pitch tent there, neither shall the shepherds make their fold there." Isa. 13:20. Nor can it be said of Babylon— "Her cities are a desolation, a dry land, and a wilderness, a land wherein no man dwells, neither do any son of man pass thereby." Jer. 51:43. Nor can it be said—" And they not take from you a stone for foundations, but you shall be desolate forever, says the Lord" (Jer. 51:26), many towns and cities have been built from the ruins of Babylon, among them four Capitol Cities,

The Battle of the Culture

Seleucia, built by Greeks; Ctesiphon, by the Parthians, Al Maiden, by the Persians; and Kufa, and by the Caliphs. Hillah was entirely constructed from the debris, and even in the houses of Bagdad, Babylonians stamped bricks may be frequently noticed. But Isaiah is still more specific for him locates the Time when his prophecy will be fulfilled. He calls it the "Day of the Lord" Isa. 13:9 That is the Millennium. And he locates it at the beginning of the Millennium, or during the events that usher in the Millennium, for he say— "The stars of heaven and the constellations thereof shall not give their light: the sun shall be darkened in the going forth, and the moon shall not cause her light to shine. Isa. 13:10 (Luke 21:25-27) surely nothing like this happened when Babylon was taken by Cyrus. In the description of the destruction of the City of Babylon given in Rev. 18 we read that her judgment will come in one hour (vs. 10), and that in one hour she shall be made desolate (vs. 19), and as an illustration of the suddenness and completeness her destruction, a mighty angel took up a stone like a Great Millstone, and cast it into the sea, saying—"Thus with Violence shall that great city Babylon be thrown and shall be found no more at all." Rev. 18:21. We are also told in the same chapter that she is to be destroyed by FIRE (Rev. 18: 8, 9, 18), and this is in exact harmony with the words of Isa. 13:19. " And Babylon, the glory of Kingdoms, the beauty of the Chaldeans excellency, shall be as whom God overthrow **Sodom and Gomorrah;"** and the Prophet Jeremiah makes the same statement. Jer. 50:40. The destruction of Sodom and Gomorrah was not protracted through many centuries, their glory disappeared in a few hours (Gen.19:24-28), and as ancient Babylon was not thus destroyed the prophesies of Isaiah and Jeremiah cannot be fulfilled unless there is to be a Future Babylon that shall be thus destroyed. In Rev. 16:17-19, we are told that Babylon shall be destroyed by an Earthquake, attended with most vivid and incessant lightning and awful thunder. It would appear then, that as Sodom and Gomorrah were first set on fire and then swallowed up by an earthquake, that the rebuilt city of Babylon will be set on fire, and as the site of ancient Babylon is under laid with Bitumen (Asphalt),

Death and Destruction

that an earthquake will break up the crust of the earth, and precipitate the burning city into a "Lake of Fire," and the city like a "Millstone" (Rev. 18 :12) sink below the surface of earth as into the sea, and be swallowed up so that it will be impossible to ever take of her stones for building purposes, and the land shall become a wilderness where no man shall ever dwell. As to the probability of the ancient city of Babylon being rebuilt we have only to consider the events that in recent years have been happening in the that part of the world looking to just such a thing. In the Department of War of France, at Paris, there is to be seen the records of valuable surveys and maps made by order of Napoleon I, in Babylonia, and among them is a plan for a New City of Babylon, thus showing that the vast schemes of Napoleon comprehended the Rebuilding of the Ancient City of Babylon, and the making it his Capitol, as his ambition was to conquer the whole of Europe and Asia, and he recognized to that end the strategically position of ancient Babylon as a governmental and commercial center. It is a fact that the whole country of Mesopotamia, Assyria and Babylonia, only needs a system of irrigation to make it again the most fertile country in the world , and steps have already been taken that direction. In 1850 the British Government sent out a military officer with his command to survey and explore the river Euphrates at a cost of at a cost of $150,000, and when the European war broke out, the great English Engineer who built the Assouam dam in Egypt, was engaged in making surveys in the Euphratean valley for the purpose of constructing a series of irrigation canals that would restore country and make it again the great grain producing country it once was. As a result towns and cities would spring up and railroads would be built. What is needed in that part of the world is a "Trans-European-Asiatic-Indian Air Line" that will connect Europe with India, and China? Such a line has been the dreams of Emperor William of Germany. It was that desire that made him and Abdul Hammed, of Turkey, the closest of political friends, and he secured from Abdul Hammed a concession to build a railway from the Asiatic side of the Bosporus, by way of Aleppo to the Tigris river, and from river, and there to Bagdad, and from Bagdad via Babylon (via Babylon, mark that)

The Battle of the Culture

to Kuwait on the Persian Gulf, and most of the road has been built to Bagdad. With these facts in mind it can readily be seen that it is the purpose of European capitalists to revive the country of Babylonia and rebuild its cities, and when once the time comes the city of Babylon will be rebuilt almost in a night and on a scale of magnificence such as the world has never seen. But I hear a protest, How you say can we be expecting Jesus to come at" any moment," if the city of Babylon must be rebuilt before He can come? There is not a word in Scripture that says that Jesus cannot come and take away His Church, until Babylon is rebuilt. The Church may be taken out of the world 25 or even 25 or even 50 years before that Babylon the Great will be an immense city, the greatest in every respect the world has ever seen. It will be a typical city, the London, the Paris, the Berlin, the Petrograd, the New York, and the Chicago of its day. It will be the greatest commercial city of the world. It will be the greatest command city of the world; Its merchandise will be of gold and silver, precious stones and pearls, of purple, and silk, and scarlet and costly wools. It's fashionable society will be clothed in the costly raiment and decked with the most costly jewels. Their homes will be filled with the most costly furniture of   precious woods, brass, iron, marble, with the richest of draperies, mats and rugs. They will use the most costly of perfumes, cinnamon, fragrant odors, ointments and frankincense; their banquets will be supplied with the sweetest of wines, the richest of pastry, and the most delicious of meats. They will have horses and chariots and the swiftest of fast moving vehicles on earth and in the air. They will have their slaves, and they will traffic in the "souls of men," that is, women will sell their bodies (prostitution) and men their souls (Homosexuality), to gratify their lusts. The markets will be crowded with cattle, sheep, and horses, the wharves will be piled with goods from all climes. The manufactories will turn out the richest of fabrics, and all that genius can invent for the comfort and convenience of men will be found on the market. It will be a city given over to pleasure and business men and promoters will give their days and nights to scheming how to make money fast and the pleasure seeking will be constantly planning new ways of pleasures.

Death and Destruction

There will be riotous joy and ceaseless feasting, as it was in the days of Noah and of Lot, they will be marrying giving in marriage, buying and selling, building and planting. The blood will run hot in their veins, money will be their god, pleasure their high-priest, and unbridled passion the ritual of their worship. It will be a city of music, amid the hustle and bustle of its commercial life will be heard the music of its pleasure resorts and theaters. There will be the sound of "harpers and musicians, of pipers and trumpeters" (vs. 22). The world's best singers and players will be there, its theaters and place of music will be going day and night. In fact there will be no night, for the electric illumination of the City by night will make the night as bright and shadowless as the day and its stores and places of business will close, night or day or Sunday for the mad whirl of pleasures and absorbing desire for riches will keep the wheels of business constantly moving. And all this will be easy because the "God of this World"—Satan will possess the minds and bodies of men, for we read in verse 2, that Babylon at that time will be "the Habitation of Devils, and the Hold of every Foul Spirit, and the Cage of Every Unclean and Hateful Bird." The city will be the seat of the most imposing "OCCULTISM," and mediums (astrology) and the those desiring to communicate with the other world (talking to the dead), will then go to Babylon, as men and women now go to Paris for fashions and sensuous pleasures. In that day demons, disembodied souls and unclean spirits will find Babylon the opportunity of their lives to materialize themselves in human bodies, and from the atmospheric heaven above, and from the Abyss below they will they come in countless legions until Babylon shall be full of demons possessed men and women, and at the height of its glory, and before and just before its fall, Babylon will be ruled by SATAN HIMSELF, incarnated in the "Beast"— ANTICHRIST. But before its destruction God will mercifully deliver His own people, for a voice from the heavens will cry— "Come Out of Her, My People, That You be Not Partakers of Her Sins, and that You Receive Not of Her Plagues." vs. 4. As Sodom and Gomorrah could not be destroyed until righteous Lot had escaped, so Babylon cannot be destroyed until all the righteous people in it have fled.

The destruction of the city will be sudden and without warning. A fearful storm will sweep over the city, the lightning and thunder will be incessant, the city will be set on fire and a great earthquake will shake it from center to circumference. The tall office buildings the "Hanging Gardens" and the great towers will tilt and fall , the crust of the earth will crack an open, and the whole city with its people will sink like a "Millstone," (vs. 21), into a lake of burning asphalts, and smoke will ascend as of a burning fiery furnace, and the horror of the scene will be so intensified by vast clouds of steam, generated by the waters of the Euphrates pouring into that lake of fiery asphalt and when night comes on those clouds of steam will reflect the light of the burning city, So it can be seen for miles in all directions in that level of the country. And the kings of the earth, and the merchants and the ship captains, and sailors, and all who have profited by her merchandise, will stand afar off and weep, and wail because of her destruction, but the heavens will rejoice for God will have rewarded her Double according to her works, and **"THE GREAT BABYLON WILL BE NO MORE"!!!!**

THE JUDGMENTS, the common opinion that the Millennium is to be ushered in by the preaching of the Gospel and that after the Millennium there is to be a "General Resurrection," followed by a "General Judgment," and then the earth is to be destroyed by fire is not scriptural. There can be no "General Judgment" because the Scriptures speak of one Judgment as being in the "Air" (1Thess. 4:16, 17: 2 Cor. 5:6-10); another on the "Earth" (Matt. 25:31-46); and a third in "Heaven," the earth and its atmosphere having fled away. Rev.20:11-15. And to make sure that these three separate Judgments should not be combined into one General Judgment scene, three different Thrones are mentioned. **1. The "Judgment Seat of Christ" 2 Cor. 5:10. "In the Air for the righteous Believers only (the Great Commissioned. Matt.28). 2. The "Throne of Glory," Matt. 25:31, 32. "On the Earth," For the "Nations," (those who had not carried out the Great Commissioned upon Christ return). 3. The "Great White Throne." Rev. 20:11, 12 "In Heaven," For the "Wicked Dead."**

Death and Destruction

The **Scriptures** speak of Five Separate Judgments they differ in five general aspects. As to "Subjects, Time, Place, Basis of Judgment and "Result." **Judgment No. 1 Subjects—Believer as to SIN. Time— A.D. 30. Place—Calvary. Basis of Judgment, Christ's "Finished Work."** Result— Death as to Christ, Justification as to the Believer. This Judgment is Past, the bible proof of the result this Judgment are Rom. 10:4. For Christ is the end of the Law for the righteousness to everyone that Believes. Christ has redeemed us from the Curse of the Law, being made a curse for us; for it is written, Cursed is every one that hangs on a tree." Gal. 3:13. "Who His own self bare our sins in His own body on the tree that we, being dead to sins, should live to righteousness." 1 Pet. 2: 24. There is therefore now no condemnation (Judgment) to them which are in Christ Jesus, who walk not after the flesh, but after the Spirit. For the Law of the Spirit of Life in Christ Jesus has made me free from the Law of "Sin and Death." Rom. 8:1, 2. "Verily, Verily, I say to you, He that hears my word, and believes on Him that sent me, Has Everlasting Life and shall not come into condemnation (Judgment) but is passed from Death to Life John 5:24. The "Believer's Judgment for Sin then is Past, and was settled at the Cross. But we must not forget that the Judgment of the Believer is threefold. 1. As a "Sinner." 2. As a "Son." 3. As a "Servant." as we have already seen his Judgment as a "Sinner" is Past. Let us look at this Judgment 2. As a "Son" as soon as the sinner accepts Christ as his personal Savior that settles the Sin question for him. For if our iniquities are laid on Him (Jesus), and then they are not on Us. Isa. 53: 5, 6. But the "Sin" question and the "Sins" question are two different things. Christ died on the Cross to atone for sin to pay the penalty of Adam's disobedience in the Garden of Eden. "Sin" is that tendency in mankind to do wrong which we call "Natural Depravity." We do not get rid of this tendency by the "New Birth," but we get a counteracting force called the "New Nature." We become a "dual personality," composed of the "Old "and "New Natures," and which all predominate depends on which we feed and which we starve.

The Battle of the Culture

This explains the "warfare" that Paul describes as his experience, after his conversion, in Rom. 7:1-25. This warfare will continue until the "Old" nature is eradicated at death "Sin" are the outward acts of wrong-doing that we commit as the result of our tendency to sin. These sins must be put away daily by "confession" My little children, these things write I to you that you sin not. And if any man sin, we have an Advocate with the Father, Jesus Christ the righteous. 1 John 2:1. "If we confess our sins, He is faithful and just to forgive us our sin and to cleanse us from all unrighteousness. 1. John 1:9. Our Judgment as "Sons" is for unconfessed sins." The Punishment is chastisement. This explains much of the chastisement of Christians, and should show them that they are "Sons" and not "Bastards" Heb. 12:5-11. Paul says— "If we would Judge ourselves we should not be judged. But when we are Judged we are chastened of the Lord, that we should not be condemned (Judged) with the world." 1 Cor. 11:31, 32. Our duty then as "Sons" is to "Self-Judge" ourselves daily, confess our sins, and so avert the Chastisement of our Heavenly Father. 3. As a Servant. This leads us to— Judgment No 2. 1. Subjects—Believers as to WORKS. 2. Time— After The Church is caught 3. Place—Judgment Seat of Christ" (in the Air) 4. Basis of Judgment—Their Works" 5. Result— Reward or loss. This Judgment is Future, We must all appear before the Judgment Seat of Christ, that every one may receive the things done in the body according to that he has done on earth, whether it be good or bad (worthless) 2 Cor. 5:10 The pronoun "We" occurs 26 times in the chapter and in every instance it mean the Believer and the Epistle is addressed to the "Church" and "Saints" at Corinth, so the Judgment here spoken of is Believers only, The "Time" of this Judgment is when the Lord comes (1Cor. 4:5), and the "Place" is in the Air (Thess. 4:17 and before the Judgment Seat of Chris)t. It will not be a Judgment in the sense of a "Trial" to see whether the Judged are innocent (saved) or guilty (lost), for it is a Judgment of the "Saved Only." It will be like the Judges stand at a Fair, or Race Track, where reward is distributed to the successful contestants. Paul describes such a scene in 1 Cor. 9:24-27.

Death and Destruction

It is not a Judgment for sin, but for "Works." This Judgment is described in 1 Cor. 3:11-15. "Our foundation can no man lay than that is laid, which is Jesus Christ. Now if any man build upon this foundation gold, silver, bronze, wood, hay or stubble; every man's works shall be made manifest; for the Day (Judgment Day) shall declare it, because it shall be revealed by fire, and the fire shall try every man's work of what sort it is. If any man's work abide which he has built there upon he shall receive a reward. If any man's work shall be burned he shall suffer loss; but he himself shall be saved; yet so as by fire. The result of this Judgment is reward or loss, all our bad and dead works, represented by wood, hay, and stubble, will be consumed, and only our good works shall remain. There is much which passes for Christian service which is merely human and secular, and does not count in our eternal reward. For those who deserve a reward it will be **"The Crowning Day."** After the Grecian games were all over the runners, wrestlers, and successful contestants assembled before the "Bema Seat "or Judges stand which was an elevated seat on which the Umpire sat and the winners received a "corruptible crown" of "laurel leaves." Some had no reward, they had lost the "Victor's Crown," But while there was no reward there was no punishment, they were not cast out. The New Testament speaks of Five Crowns. 1. **The Crown of "Life."** This is the "Martyrs" crown, and is mentioned twice. "Blessed is the man that endures temptation (testing), for when he is tried (at the Judgment Seat of Christ), he shall receive the Crown of Life which the Lord has promised to them that loves Him." James 1:12 "Fear none of those things which you shall suffer; behold, the Devil shall cast some of you into prison, that you may be tried (tested) and you shall have tribulation ten days; you be faithful to death, and I will give you a crown of Life." Rev. 2:20. Notice it does not say until death but to death. They were not to recant but to remain faithful to a Martyr's death, to recant was to lose the crown. (The Nations) This refers to the martyrs of the Tribulation Period. 2. **The "Crown of Glory."** This is the Elder's or Pastors crown, given by the Chief shepherd when He shall appear. But it is not for those who serve for "filthy lucre" (dirty money) or "lord it over God's heritage. 1 Pet. 5:2-4.

The Battle of the Culture

3. **The "Crown of Rejoicing,"** this is the "Soul Winner's" crown. Those brought to Jesus by us will be our "Crown of Rejoicing" at His Coming. 1 Thess. 2: 19, 20. Phil. 4:1. (The righteous believer carrying out the Great Commission)

4. **The "Crown of Righteousness,"** this is the crown of those who love His appearing and will be given in that day—the Day of His Appearing (the Church —Rapture), 2 Tim. 4:8.

5. **The "Crown of Incorruptible,"** this is the "Victor's Crown" and is for those who keep under their body. 1 Cor. 9: 25-27. Who do not yield to their fleshly lusts? Who do not permit themselves to be diverted from the Master's work by worldly amusements and pleasures, nor saturate their bodies with drugs? If we do not want to be ashamed at His Coming, 1 John 2: 28, let us see to it that we keep our body under and so live that we shall secure a crown. (The 144,000). **Judgment No. 3.** 1. Subjects— The Jews. 2. Time—The Great Tribulation. 3. Place—Jerusalem and Vicinity. 4. Basis of Judgment—Rejection of the Godhead. 5. Result—Their Conversion and Reception of Christ as Their Messiah. The Judgment is Future while Church is being judged at the Judgment Seat of Christ in the Air the Jews will be judged under Antichrist on earth. The Jews are an earthly people and as all the promises to them are earthly, it follows that their Judgment must be of an earthly character. The basis of their Judgment is their rejection of the Godhead. In the days of Samuel they rejected God the Father. I Sam. 8:7. In the days of Christ they rejected God the Son. Luke 23:18. In the days of Christ they rejected God the Son. Luke. 23:18. In the days of Stephen they rejected God the Holy Spirit. Act 7:51, 54-60. For their sin they been scattered among the nations until the Times of the Gentiles are fulfilled. When the Times of the Gentiles are about to end the Jews will be gathered back to the Holy Land unconverted and caused to pass under the rod. Ez. 20:34-38. They will be cast into God's Melting Pot (Ez. 22:19-22), and pass through an experience spoken of by Jeremiah and Daniel as the Times of Jacobs Trouble. Jer. 30:4-7, Dan. 12:1. Christ calls it The Great Tribulation, and He and Zechariah the Prophet associate it with the Return of the Lord.

Death and Destruction

Matt. 24:21-31. Zech. 14:11. The human agent the Lord will use will be Antichrist, the awfulness of whose rule will be supplemented by the pouring out of the Vials of God's wrath upon the earth. Rev. 15:1, 5-8; 16:21. The result of these terrible Judgments will be that the Jews will call in their misery upon the Lord. Zech. 12:1`0. Then Christ will come back to the Mt. of Olives (Zech. 14:3) and the Jews will look upon him whom they pierced (Zech. 12:10) and a nation, the Jewish Nation, shall be born (converted) in a day. Isa. 66:8. **Judgment No 4.** 1, Subjects—The Nations (Gentiles). 2. Time—the Revelation of Christ. 3. Place—The Throne of His Glory, On the Earth —Valley of Jehoshaphat. 4. Basis of Judgment—Their Treatment of Christ's Brethren—the Jews. 5. Result—Some Nations "Saved," others destroyed. This Judgment is Future. The account of this Judgment is given in Matt. 25:31-46. The description of this Judgment and of one given in Rev. 20:11-15 are combined by many, and taken to teach the doctrine of a general Judgment. But when he compares them, they differ so widely, that it is evident that they do not describe the same event. What God has put asunder let no man join together. The following comparison will show the difference in the two accounts. **Matt. 25:31-46.** 1. No Resurrection. 2. Living Nation Judged. 3. on the Earth. Joel. 3:2 4. No Books Mentioned. 5. Three Classes Named Sheep, Goat and Brethren. 6. Time—Before the Millennium. **Rev. 20:11-15.** 1. A Resurrection. 2. Dead Judged. 3. Heaven and Earth Gone. 4. Books Open. 5. One class Named. "The Dead." 6. Time—After the Millennium.   This comparison reveals the fact that one of these Judgments is on Earth, the other in the heavens, and they are separated by a 1000 years. The Greek word "ethnos" here translated "Nations" occurs 158 times in the New Testament. It is translated Gentiles 92 times, "Nation" or "Nations" 61 times, and the Heathen 5 times, but it is never in any instance (unless it be this) applied either to the dead or the resurrected. As this is a Judgment of Nations only, the Jews cannot be in it, for they are not reckoned among the Nations. Num. 23:9. And as the Church will be associated with Christ in this Judgment for the "Saints" (Church) shall Judge the world (the Nations), (1Cor 6:2), the Church cannot be in this Judgment either.

The Battle of the Culture

As we have seen the Church and the Jews have already been judged, so the Judgment of the Nations cannot be a general Judgment. Who then, is ask, are meant by the Sheep? Do they not represent the Righteous and all the righteous from the beginning of the world to the end of Time? And do not the Goat in like manner represent all the wicked? If the Sheep are the righteous and the Goat the Wicked, then who are the Brethren? If they are the followers of Christ, as some claim, they should be class with the Sheep. The Scripture teaches that the righteous are saved by "faith," and the Wicked are the lost because they "reject Christ," but in this Judgment scene the Sheep inherit "Kingdom" and the Goats are commanded to depart, because of their treatment of the Brethren. All the confusion is caused by trying to make a Judgment of nations mean a Judgment of individuals. The Sheep represent one class of Nations, and the Goat another class, while the Brethren represent the Jews (Christ's Brethren). We must bear in mind the time and place of the Judgment. The time is at the "Revelation of Christ," when He comes to set up His Millennial Kingdom on the earth. The place is the Valley of Jehoshaphat in the vicinity of Jerusalem. "For behold in those days, and in that time, when I shall bring again the captivity of Judah and Jerusalem, I will gather all nations and will bring them down into the valley of Jehoshaphat, and will plead with them there for my people and for my heritage Israel. Whom they have scattered among the Nations, parted my Land Joel 3:1, 2. This prophecy clearly states that there is to be a Judgment of Nations on the earth of the "Valley of Jehoshaphat," at the time of the restoration of the Jews to their own land, and that the basis of Judgment is the treatment by the Nations of Christ's Brethren—the Jews. During the "Tribulation Period," the Nations that treat the Jewish people kindly, feeding and clothing them and visiting them in prison, will be the "Sheep Nations" while those who neglect to do so will be the "Goat Nations." At the Judgment of Nations the King (Christ) will say to the Sheep Nations," In as much as you have been kind to my Brethren (the Jews) Come, you blessed of my Father, inherit the Kingdom prepared for you from the foundation of the world.

Death and Destruction

This Kingdom is the "Millennial Kingdom" that the "Sheep Nations" as Nations will inherit and posses during the Millennium. And they are to be among the saved "Nations" of the New Earth (Rev. 21: 24) it can be said of them that they, or at least the righteous individuals in them, shall enter into Life eternal. Matt. 25:46. Christ sentence upon the Goat nation will be depart from me, you cursed into everlasting fire, prepared for the Devil and his angels, and these shall go away into everlasting punishment." The Goat Nations will at once be destroyed as Nations, not one of them shall get into the Millennium, and the wicked individuals that compose them will perish and be eternally lost. **Judgment No. 5.** 1. Subject—The Wicked Dead. 2. Time—During the Renovation of the Earth by Fire. 3. Place—before the Great white Throne. 4. Basis of Judgment—Their Works." 5. Result—Cast into the Lake of Fire." The account of it is given in Rev. 20:11-15. It will take place at the close of the Millennium 1000 years after the Judgment of the Nations, and before the Great White Throne. The Great White Throne will not be on earth, for the Great white Throne Judgment will take place during the Renovation of the earth by fire, for the renovation of the Earth is reserved or kept until the time of that Judgment, which Peter calls the "Day of Judgment" and Perdition of Ungodly men(2 Pet. 3:7). Because the Judgment of the Great White Throne is the Judgment of the Wicked dead. All the righteous dead will rise at the first resurrection. If any righteous die between the first Resurrection and the Resurrection of the wicked or second Resurrection, they will rise with the wicked dead at the Resurrection. The words—"Whosoever was not found written in the Book of Life (vs. 15), implies that there will be some, probably very few, Righteous at the second Resurrection. At the close of the Millennium and just before the renovation of the earth by fire, the living righteous will probably be translated and the living Wicked or Ungodly will be destroyed in the flames that will consume the earth's atmosphere and exterior surface. The Wicked or Ungodly will not be Judged to see whether they are entitled to Eternal Life, but to ascertain the degree of their punishment.

The Battle of the Culture

The sad feature of this Judgment will be that there will be many kind and loveable people there who were not saved, and who will be classed among the ungodly because they rejected Christ as their Savior. The Books will be open in which the Recording Angel have kept a record of every person's life, and they will judge every man according to his works. Some will be sentence to a more severe punishment than others, but none will escape. The worse of all is, that those who were not so bad will spend eternity with the ungodly, and that in the Lake of Fire," their punishment includes the second death, which means that they shall lose their resurrection bodies, in which they were judged and became disembodied spirits again, and so exist in the "Lake of Fire" Forever. The "Fallen Angels" (not the Devils angels), who are reserved in everlasting chains under darkness, will be judged at this time, which Jude calls the "Judgment of the Great Day." Jude 6. When this Judgment is over the Devil and his angels, and all the ungodly, will have been consigned to the "Lake of Fire," and the Universe purged of all evil, and righteousness shall reign supreme on the New Earth.

CHAPTER VIII

SIGNS

OF

THE TIMES

While we cannot name the exact date of the Lord's Return its nearness may be known character of the Times. As to this the New Testament gives no uncertain sound. In Dan. 12:4, 9-10, we read, "But you, O Daniel, shut the words and seal the Book, even to the "Time of the End," many shall run to and fro, and knowledge shall be increased. . . Go your way, Daniel: for the words are closed up sealed till the Time of the End. Many shall be purified, and made white, and tried; but the wicked shall do wickedly; and none of the wicked shall understand; but the "Wise Shall Understand." These words declare that the prophecies of Daniel were to be "shut up" and "sealed" until the "Time of The End." The expression does not mean the "end of Time," but is the angelic messenger's way of referring to the "Last Days" of the "Times of the Gentiles." At which time he declares that the Book will be "unsealed," and "knowledge shall be increased."

The Battle of the Culture

What is here meant is "prophetic knowledge" of the things recorded in the Book of Daniel and other prophetic writings of the Scriptures. This is made clear by the statement that only the "wise" shall understand. That is, who are enlightened by the Holy Spirit, and not those who merely intellectual knowledge, for the wicked shall not understand, how wonderfully this is true of these days. The Higher Critics have labored hard to discredit the Book of Daniel, but without avail, for the Book is more studied than ever, and is being "unsealed" by Holy Spirit enlightened students of the Word of God, who clearly see that we have reached the "Time of the End," and are living in the closing days of the "Time of the Gentiles." The "unsealing" began about 100 years ago, when the "Midnight Cry," Behold, the Bridegroom Comes," was heard in the "Revival of Premillennial Truth." For centuries while the Bridegroom tarried the Wise and Foolish virgins "All slumbered and slept." and the Church lapsed into a condition of spiritual apathy, and "The Blessed Hope" was eclipsed. But now all over the world the blessed Hope has emerged from the shadow, and the virgins are "Trimming their lamps" preparatory to going out to meet their Lord, but only the "wise" have oil in their vessels and in their lamps. We are now living in the "Fourth Watch of the Night," soon the "Morning Star" (Christ. Rev. 22:16) will appear and we shall be caught out at the Rapture to meet Him and go into the Marriage Feast. Here we glance at the 'Signs of the Times: 1. POST-MILLENNIAL SCOFFERS, in 2 Pet. 3:3-4 we read, "That there shall come in the Last Day's Scoffers, walking after their own lust, and saying, Where is the promise of His coming? For since the fathers fell asleep, all things continue as they from the beginning of the creation." How true this is of the present day. The Doctrine of the Second Coming is "scoffed" at, and those whose hold it are looked upon as deluded fanatics, and sad to say, this opposition comes from prominent religious leaders of the day. 2. APOSTASY. In 2 Thess 2:3, we told that "That Day" (the day of the Lord) shall not come, except there come a Falling Away first.

Sign of the Time

This Falling Away is evidenced on every hand. 3. FALSE TEACHERS, in 2 Pet. 2;1-2 we are warned against "False Teachers" who shall privately bring in "damnable heresies," even denying the Lord that bought them, such as Christian Scientists and that many shall follow their pernicious ways, and sad to relate these followers are recruited from the orthodox church members, of whom the Apostle Paul wrote to Timothy (2 Tim 4:3-4), saying: The time will come when they will not endure sound doctrine; but after their own lusts they heap to themselves teachers, having after their own lusts shall they heap to themselves teachers, having itching ears; and they shall turn away their ears from the truth, and shall be turned to Fables. This turning away is evidenced on every hand. There is a "turning away" in doctrinal standards, in the demand for a regenerated church membership, in church and Sunday school attendance, and in Sabbath observance. Many churchgoers will not endure "sound doctrine." They will not go to hear those who preach the total depravity of man, the necessity of the "New Birth," and the conscious and endless torment of those who reject Christ as a personal Savior. They demand teachers who will "itch" (tickle) their ears with pleasing, novel and sensational doctrines.

4. SPIRITUALISM, in 1 Tim. 4:1 we are warned of a departure from the faith. That in the "Latter Times" (the Last Days of this Dispensation), some shall "depart from the faith, giving heed to seducing spirits and doctrines of devils." This is being fulfilled in the increasing number of those who are forsaking their Christian belief to become followers of Spiritualistic Mediums and to dabble in Psychical Research. 5. PERILOUS TIMES, of these times Paul told Timothy, This knows also, that in the Last Days perilous Times shall come. For men shall be lovers of their own selves, covetous, boasters, proud, blasphemers, disobedient to parents, unthankful, unholy, without natural affection (for their own offspring), true breakers, false accusers, incontinent, fierce, despisers of those who are good, traitors, heady, high minded, lover of pleasures more than lovers of God; having a Form of godliness, but denying the Power thereof. 2 Tim. 3:1-5

we have neither time nor space to enlarge upon the above, but what's catalogue we have of the "perilous conditions" of the times in which we live. 6. HEADED UP TRESURE, in James 5:1-6, we are told that in the Last Days there shall be a class of rich men who shall have Heaped treasures together and that by Fraud and who shall use their ill-gotten gain in the pursuit of "pleasure" and "wantonness, and that God will hear the cry of those who have been cheated of their just share of the profits, and will send a sore judgment upon the guilty. What a description we have here of the unprincipled, speculative and profiteering spirit of the days in which we live, when men become millionaires, and multi-millionaires, in a few years. Truly we are living in the "Last Days" of this Dispensation. 7. A LAODICEAN CHURCH, in the Message to the Church of Laodicea (Rev. 3:14-22) we have a description of the last stage of the professing Church on earth. It is described as neither "hot" nor "cold," but nauseatingly lukewarm, so that Christ says He will "spit it out of His Mouth." It boastingly will claim to be "Rich" and "Increased with goods" and to have a "need for nothing," not even of Christ, for He will be excluded and will have to knock for admittance, and it will be ignorant of its true condition, that it is wretched, and miserable, and poor, and blind an naked. Unspeakably sad it is that this is the condition to a large extent of professing Church of today. 8. THE-FIG TREE SIGN, when Jesus Disciples asked Him, after He had foretold the destruction of the Temple: Tell us, when shall these things be? And what shall be the sign of the coming, and of the end of the world (Age)? (Matt. 24:1-3), Jesus gave as a "Sign" of His Coming the "Fig-Tree Sign." The "Fig-Tree" symbolizes the nation of Israel, and its "budding" the revival of Israel as a nation. Here again we have evidence of the nearness of the Lord's Return for the revival of Zionism, and the passing of the Land of Palestine onto the hands of a Christian nation, opens the way for the restoration of the Jews to their own land, and the fulfillment of the Fig-Tree Sign. The fact that the city of Jerusalem surrendered without the firing of a shot is significant.

Sign of the Time

Jesus said that Jerusalem was to be trodden down of the Gentiles until "The Time of the Gentiles" should be fulfilled (Luke 21:24), and the taking of Jerusalem at this time may signify that "The Times of the Gentiles" is drawing to close. 9. THE DISTRESS OF NATIONS, IN Luke 21:24-27 Jesus tells us that as the "Times of the Gentiles" come to a close, "there shall be signs in the sun, and in the moon, and in the stars; and upon the earth Distress of Nations, with perplexity; the sea and the waves (the peoples of the earth) roaring; men's hearts failing them for fear, and for looking after those things which are coming on the earth: for the Power of Heaven (the Principalities and Powers of Evil, Eph. 6:11-12), shall be shaken. And then shall they see the Son of man coming in a cloud with power and great glory. In the prophecy of Haggai 2:6-7, we read: "Thus says the Lord of hosts; yet once, it is a little while, and I will shake the heavens and the earth, and the sea, and the dry land; and I will Shake All Nations, and the Desire (Christ) Of All Nations Will Come." This has never been fulfilled as yet, and the present "Distress of the Nations," the uprising of the masses in "National Revolutions," the "Tottering Thrones" and other indications that the nations are being shaken, is still further proof the we are living in the Times— just preceding appearing of the Son of Man, the Desire of All Nations, who will bring peace to this troubled Earth. 10. NOAHS DAYS, which last "sign:" that we would mention is the sign of the days of Noah's. Luke 17:26-30 As it was in the days of Noah, they did eat, they drank, they married wives, they were given in marriage, they brought, they sold, they planted, they build, so shall it be in the days of the Son of Man. Where, you say, is the sin in doing these thing?. They are not only commanded, they are necessary. That is true, the sin was not in "doing" them, but in them "Until the Flood came," That is, they did nothing else. They forgot to worship their Maker, so today men and women are so busily engaged in doing the good things of life that they have no time to worship God. They are so busy building homes for themselves on earth that they are neglecting to secure a home in heaven.

The Battle of the Culture

They are more anxious that their children should make a good match, or mothers continue to baby sit their sons into adulthood, rather than be united and maintain their relationship to the Lord and Savior. The Men have forgotten their position of being the Foundation of the Family, the women have not received the knowledge of a Helpmeet to her husband. They are so much concerned about their business on the Job or case in Court that they have forgotten that they must stand at the Judgment Seat of **GOD!**

Dear reader, are you a Christian, and as a Christian are you a believer in the "Blessed Hope," and are you looking for the speedy coming of the Lord, and doing all you can to hasten His Return, and thus bring back The King? If not, I beseech you to drop everything, "stop questioning God" and settle the question of whether you will be "caught up" to meet the Lord in the air when He comes, and thus escape the awful days that are coming on earth—days in which no one can have that "Mark" are eternally doomed. Rev. 13:15-17.

"HE SHALL COME,"

What I say to you I say to all, Watch, At Evening, At Midnight, At the Cock-Crowing," it may be in the evening, when the work of the day is done, and you have time to sit in the twilight, and to watch the sinking sun; while the long bright day dies slowly Over the sea, and the hour grows quiet and holy with thoughts of Me; while you hear the village children passing along the street, among these thronging footsteps May come the sound of My feet; Therefore I tell you, watch! By the light of the evening star, When the room is growing dusky As the clouds afar; Let the door be on the latch In your home, For it may be through the gloaming, I will come. It may be in the midnight when 'tis heavy upon the land, And the black wave lying dumbly along the sand; when the moonless night draws close And the lights are out in the house, When the fires burn low and red, And the watch is ticking loudly Beside the bed; Though you sleep tired on your couch, Still your heart must wake and watch In the dark room; For it may be that at midnight I will come. It may be at the cock-crow, When the night is dying slowly In the sky, And the sea looks calm and holy, Waiting for the dawn of the golden sun Waiting for the dawn of the golden sun, Which draws nigh; When the mists are on the valleys, shading, The river chill, And my morning star is fading, fading Over the hill; Behold, I say to you watch! Let the door be on the latch in your home, In the chill before the dawning, Between the night and morning, I may come. It may be in the morning When the sun is bright and strong, And the dew is glittering sharply Over the little lawn When the waves are laughing loudly Along the shore, And the little birds are singing sweetly About the little birds are singing sweetly About the door; With the long days work before you, You are up with the sun, and the neighbors come to talk a little Of all that must be done; But, remember, that I may be the next To come in at the door, To call you from your busy work, For evermore.

As you work, your heart must watch, for the door is on the latch in your room, and it may be in the morning I will come. So I am watching quietly Every day, Wherever the sun shines brightly I rise and say, Surely it is the shining of His Face, And look to the gates of the His High place Beyond the sea, For I know He is coming shortly To summon me; And when a shadow falls across the window Of my room, Where I am working my appointed task, I lift my head to watch the door and ask If He has come! And the Spirit answers softly In my home, "Only a few more shadows, And He will Come!

— The Unseen.—

A MESSAGE TO THE CHURCH

THE MIISION OF THE CHURCH, As we have seen the Church is not an "Organization" but an "Organism." Therefore it is not a "Social Club," organized and supported solely for the benefit of its members. It is not a "Place of Amusement" to pander to the carnal nature of man. It is not a "Concert Hall full of song and dance movements Only." It is not a "House of Merchandise" for sale of "Indulgences," or other commodities, whereby the money of the ungodly can be secured and save penurious church member a little self sacrifice. Neither is it a "Reform Bureau" to save the "bodies" of men. The reformation of men is very commendable, as are all forms of "Social Service," but that is not the work or mission of the Church. The world was just as full, if not fuller, of the evils that afflict society today, in the days of Christ, but He never, nor did the Apostles, organize any reform agencies. He knew that the source of all the evils in the world is SIN, and the only way to eradicate sin is to regenerate the Human Heart, and so He gave to the world The Gospel, and the Mission of the Church is to carry that Gospel to the Whole World (The Four Corners of the Earth). Mark 16:15.

The Gospel is not a system of "Ethics," or a "Code of Morals," it is a

Proclamation of Salvation. "I am not ashamed of the **Gospel of Christ** for it is the Power of GOD to Salvation to everyone that Believes To the Jew First and Also To The Gentile (The Nation and The Jews)." Rom. 1:16. The purpose of the Gospel in this Dispensation is not to Save Society, but to save the Individual Members that are to compose the "Body of Christ"—THE CHURCH. The great mistake the Church has made is in appropriating to herself, in this Dispensation, the promises of earthly conquest and glory which belong exclusively to Israel in Millennial, or "Kingdom Age." As soon as the Church enters into an "Alliance with the World," and seeks the help of Parliaments, or Government, Congress, Legislatures, and Reform Societies largely made up of ungodly men and women, she loses her spiritual power and becomes helpless as a **REDEEMING FORCE!**

20 TIME AUTHOR

INSPIRATIONAL/MOTIVATIONAL

EVANGELICAL SPEAKER

PHOTO BY DREAM PHOTO
WWW.DREAMPHOTOUS.COM

www.ingramcontent.com/pod-product-compliance
Lightning Source LLC
Chambersburg PA
CBHW021843220426
43663CB00005B/385